Auditing With The Computer

Publications of the Institute of
Business and Economic Research

Recent publications in this series:

A THEORY OF ACCOUNTING TO INVESTORS
by George L. Staubus (1961)

ORGANIZATION, AUTOMATION, AND SOCIETY
by Robert A. Brady (1961)

HOUSING POLICY—THE SEARCH FOR SOLUTIONS
by Paul F. Wendt (1962)

COMPETITION, REGULATION, AND
THE PUBLIC INTEREST IN NONLIFE INSURANCE
by Roy J. Hensley (1962)

PUBLIC ENTERPRISE ECONOMICS
AND TRANSPORT PROBLEMS
by Tillo E. Kuhn (1962)

ASSET PRICES IN ECONOMIC ANALYSIS
by Samuel B. Chase, Jr. (1963)

THE SIX-LEGGED DOG—MATTEI AND ENI:
A STUDY IN POWER
by Dow Votaw (1964)

A HISTORY OF RUSSIAN ECONOMIC THOUGHT:
NINTH THROUGH EIGHTEENTH CENTURIES
by John M. Letiche (1964)

RAILROAD MERGERS AND ABANDONMENTS
by Michael Conant (1964)

INTER-ECONOMY COMPARISONS: A CASE STUDY
by Leonard A. Doyle (1965)

AUDITING WITH
THE COMPUTER

Wayne S. Boutell

PUBLICATIONS OF THE INSTITUTE OF BUSINESS AND
ECONOMIC RESEARCH • UNIVERSITY OF CALIFORNIA

UNIVERSITY OF CALIFORNIA PRESS
BERKELEY AND LOS ANGELES
1965

University of California Press
Berkeley and Los Angeles, California

Cambridge University Press
London, England

TO YVONNE

Preface

The future of the computer in business operations is very bright. However, this is not an unmixed blessing: as business data-processing systems rapidly become more complex, the problems of control multiply at an even greater pace. The development and control of business-oriented computer systems are separate problems which suggest conflicting solutions. The logical objective is to maintain some sort of balance between the technological innovations and the use of acceptable control criteria.

The purpose of this book is twofold: (1) to examine the environment within which business data-processing systems function, and (2) to explore possible solutions to the problems which the auditor faces in reviewing these systems. The auditing profession is at a crossroads. We can either inhibit change by demanding adequate safeguards in terms of familiar evidence, or we can attempt to seek new ways of reviewing business data-processing systems which will not interfere with technical progress.

Much of the discussion which has centered around this problem has been at a theoretical level. The chief difficulty with dealing with the issue in the abstract is that doing so focuses the effort on attempting to evolve general criteria that may be applicable to all business data-processing systems. Unfortunately, these attempts cannot possibly succeed in any meaningful sense, as we do not have an underlying generally accepted theory of business information systems. Since business data-processing systems are not homogeneous, the auditing procedures and techniques applicable to these systems must also vary.

The methodology employed in this presentation combines what has been said and done in the past with some suggestions of what should be done in the future to attempt a reconciliation between developmental and control criteria for business systems. My basic dissatisfaction with the situation several years ago (which dissatisfaction, on the whole, persists today) gave rise to an exploratory study, including development of an experimental computer model, in connection with a course that I was taking in preparation for my doctoral qualifying examinations. This original study led to two years of additional research and study in connection with the writing of a doctoral dissertation on the subject.

This present work retains some of the ideas I developed in those earlier studies, but also adds the perspective that comes with time. It is evident to me that this attempt is merely the first in a long progression of studies on the subject—studies sorely needed in our present dilemma.

This study would not have been possible without the support and encouragement of my colleagues on the faculty of the School of Business Administration at the University of California, Berkeley. In particular, I would like to express my appreciation for the encouragement and assistance of Professor William J. Vatter in the review of numerous drafts and revisions. Professor Austin C. Hoggatt provided valuable suggestions in reviewing the computer programs and in criticism of the manuscript. Professor Mason Haire of the Department of Psychology aided in the development of the survey questionnaire and in the preliminaries of the organizational aspects of the study. The facilities of the Computer Center of the University of California were of vital importance in developing and "debugging" the computer programs.

A Doctoral Dissertation Fellowship sponsored by the Arthur Andersen & Co. Foundation initially underwrote my research. The assistance provided by the partners and staff of Arthur Andersen & Co. was most helpful in obtaining a perspective of current practices. Publication of the study is sponsored by the Institute of Business and Economic Research at the University of California, Berkeley.

In view of the rapid developments in computer technology as related to auditing procedures, it is perhaps appropriate to remind the reader that references to "at present" throughout this text indicate the date below.

W. S. BOUTELL

Berkeley, California
June, 1964

Contents

I. Introduction   1

II. The Business Information System   9

III. The Development of the Business-Oriented Computer   23

IV. Auditing in a Changing Environment   46

V. Auditing Theory and Practice   60

VI. Auditing "Through the Computer"   83

VII. The Future of the Business-Oriented Computer and Its Impact on Auditing Theory and Practice   99

Appendix A: Survey Questionnaire and Summary of Responses   109

Appendix B: Computer Audit Program for Test of a Factory Payroll   125

Appendix C: Computer Audit Program for the Test of an Order-Billing System   147

Bibliography   175

I

Introduction

Since the introduction of the computer into the business firm in the mid-1950's, there has been considerable emphasis on the design of information systems which are economically efficient. The relatively high cost of computer installations requires that sizable savings be realized in order to justify the changeover costs. Until fairly recently the control criteria applicable to a well-balanced system were considered to be artificially imposed restrictions inhibiting the design of efficient computer systems. Computer manufacturers have incorporated into their equipment appropriate controls insuring processing accuracy, but they have not been concerned with the external controls which govern the relationship between the computer equipment and the rest of the business organization. The auditing profession has attempted to bridge this gap by assuming that evidence obtained by conventional auditing methods would provide sufficient assurances that the computer system was, in fact, operating within the framework of acceptable control standards. Unfortunately, this approach has tended to restrict the systems designer in his efforts to obtain the most efficient system possible within a given set of circumstances.

This study examines the underlying forces which contribute to the problems which the auditor faces today. Briefly stated, the forces which have been identified fall into three broad categories: (1) the concept of a business information system; (2) the technological developments in computer hardware; and (3) the dynamic aspects of auditing theory. The conflict between efficient system design and adequate control procedures forms the central theme of the discussion in the first part of the book. It is hoped that the suggestions offered in chapters v and vi will provide a starting point for additional critical and constructive thinking concerning adequate control procedures for business-oriented computer systems. I began my study assuming that the development and control aspects of data-processing systems can be reconciled, and my work has reinforced that belief.

Traditionally, the role of the certified public accountant has been to review the activities of a business firm in retrospect. This makes it rather difficult to assess the impact of current developments in business organization when auditing theory and practice lag behind current changes in organization. Fortunately, there have been changes recently in the organization of the public accounting firm itself; these have tended to reduce the lag between changes occurring in the business firm and the attendant shifts in auditing theory and practice. One of the important changes has been the rise of the management services function of the public accounting firm. Beyond the traditional auditing services, clients have come to expect and demand constructive suggestions and assistance in developing and improving their business information systems. The public accounting profession, in response to this pressure, has begun to add to its skills some technical competence for dealing with a great many of the problems of the system itself. In some cases, admittedly few at the present time, the public accountant actually has the responsibility for shaping and implementing the business information system. Another important change has involved an explicit attempt to equalize the audit work load over the calendar year, an arrangement which further commends the shift in emphasis from the *ex post facto* approach to the examination of the business information system itself. Finally, the gradual evolution of a management-type report to accompany the formal audit report has increased the need for auditors who can constructively criticize an existing business system.

Always bearing in mind the limitations of viewing the business firm from the standpoint of the professional auditor, this analysis is directed primarily toward the individual firm, and from that perspective investigates the present practices of the public accounting profession in the light of current developments in business information systems, attempts to formulate a theoretical framework underlying those practices; and suggests a solution for establishing controls over the business information system which, although admittedly limited, will indicate the direction in which future efforts should be directed.

In order to accomplish the first two objectives, it is necessary to examine the influences which have shaped the environment within which the business firm presently functions. Accordingly, chapter ii deals in detail with the question of what comprises a business information system. As will be fully explained there, a business information system can be considered to be a particular aspect of the broader notion of the theory of the business firm. The auditor traditionally has been concerned with only that part of a business information system which deals with internal accounting controls. As progressive public accounting firms are beginning to realize, another very important aspect of a business information system involves the interaction of all functional areas of the firm, such as production, marketing, and personnel. Not only must systems be reviewed by the practitioner, but he must be ready to suggest the type of business information system which would be the most desirable in a particular set of circumstances. At present, some theoretical norms are needed to provide a frame of reference for designing an efficient system in a given case.

Considerable study has been devoted to the concept of a system; unfortunately, accountants are not in the forefront of this activity. By and large, they have passively adopted a pedestrian approach to the systems concept, and only on rare occasions do they even consider, or seem aware of, the total systems concept. Where then can theoretical concepts be found? Electrical engineering provides a starting point for the investigation, but it soon proves to be somewhat sterile because of the lack of behavioral variables in the description of the system. Operations research contributes some useful ideas to the systems concept, but the field is split as to the proper approach to be taken in a given situation. Current studies in organization theory shed additional light on the problem and recent works in this field provide valuable insights into the problem of systems and systems design. Finally, there is the concept of a system as it is to be found, explicitly or implicitly, in current business information practice. This is extremely important because, as public accounting firms participate more and more in the design and implementation of business information systems, past experience furnishes the foundation for further developments.

In 1954, one electronic computer was in use processing business transactions. By July 1, 1962, according to the best estimates available, approximately 6,000 electronic computers were in use in business. By the end of 1963, the 1962 number had more than doubled. And—it is almost too well known to mention—the decade saw vast advances in the versatility, velocity, and volume of the computer's capacity. Chapter iii is devoted to a brief review of the major technological developments pertinent to the rapid acceptance of the business-oriented computer. In this regard, it is significant that the initial development of the electronic computer occurred almost entirely in response to the need for better ways of accumulating, calculating, and summarizing scientific, engineering, and statistical data. The needs of business were not considered. The use of the computer for scientific purposes often requires a relatively small amount of input, large computing capacity, and perhaps a simple statement as output. Consequently, the rather different requirements for business information systems have led to the development of specifically business-oriented computers more recently.

As the potential for the use of the electronic computer has been increasingly recognized by the business community, the marked disparity between the speeds of the central processor and the input-output equipment has become of increasing concern to equipment manufacturers. Business data processing normally requires high-volume input and high-volume output, with relatively little emphasis on the speed or logical capacity of the central processor. As a result of the burgeoning demands of business firms, developments in peripheral equipment have occurred with bewildering speed since 1960. The central processors, on the other hand, have remained relatively unchanged. Perhaps the greatest single roadblock to the development of integrated data-processing systems has been the functional imbalance of equipment installations. These problems as well as their source—the character of the equipment currently available to business firms—comprise a critical aspect of the business environment in which the accountant currently works. It is especially important to understand this environment because the already tremendous impact of electronic data-processing equipment will continue to increase in the next decade, and future technological developments depend to a great extent on our appreciation of past and present problems.

Chapter iv reviews the development of auditing theory and practice from their early beginnings up to the present date. Auditing theory has long been highly influenced by the demands of the business community. Auditing has traditionally implied a review of a past transaction or event and an independent judgment as to its implication, authenticity, or fairness. Early laws in England required the auditor to perform an attest function as to the correctness of balance sheets submitted for joint stock companies, other parliamentary companies, and railroads. The Securities and Exchange Commission in the United States requires an opinion by independent public accountants on the financial statements of companies registered on the major stock exchanges. Although these legal demands guide and enforce auditing requirements, the demands of the business community have in fact always preceded action by the legislative bodies. Pressures on the auditing profession have come from bankers, stockholders, labor unions, suppliers, and consumers. The trend of auditing theory can be directly traced to the requirements of these various interest groups; in many instances the result has been legislation to influence auditing standards and procedures. The history of auditing theory is specifically important to the present analysis of the role of the certified public accountant in the business community since innovations in that role cannot be sanctioned directly by historical precedents which were until recently the primary guidelines to the conduct of the examination of financial statements.

Auditing theory, while greatly influenced by the emerging concept of the business information system and its attendant technical developments, as well as by historical auditing precedents, must concern itself with the impact of these forces on present practices within the profession. Accordingly, chapter v is a study of the impact of auditing theory, business information systems, and electronic computers on the business community—all from the viewpoint of the public accounting practitioner. The literature on auditing using electronic data-processing systems has not been very extensive, and what has been written is confusing to the practitioner as well as to the data-processing specialist. The literature gives the impression that unless the auditor immediately acquires an extensive knowledge of the technical aspects of the business-oriented computer, he will be unable to express an opinion on the financial statements of the business firm which uses this equipment. The almost universal reaction of auditing theorists and practitioners, therefore, has been to insist upon the maintenance of traditional records so that auditing procedures can remain substantially unchanged. The auditing profession hoped by means of this stop-gap procedure to forestall the day when all auditors must become experts in electronic equipment. This approach certainly tends to retard the efficient use of business-oriented computers and is detrimental to development of integrated data-processing systems. The literature generally recognizes this problem, but it confuses three separate phases of development, and this confusion gives rise to conflicting opinions and uncertainty.

The principal error appears to be a failure to consider the time dimension appropriately. For example, in some instances the installation of a business-oriented computer results in little or no change in the basic accounting techniques and procedures from those which exist when electric accounting machines (EAM) or manual systems are used. This is particularly true in the case of the IBM 1401 card-oriented computer. The basic notion of systems planners and equipment manufacturers appears to be to use the computer as a substitute for various time-consuming functions traditionally performed by accounting clerks. Writers on the subject fail to recognize that this phase already shows signs of becoming obsolete. The advent of the tape-oriented computer system leads to a number of new concepts for information storage and retrieval which did not exist in the card-oriented systems. This second phase of development will undoubtedly be followed by a third, in which the conventional movement from source document to report will be made superfluous by the elimination of the source document from the data-processing system. This phase will also involve a concept of mass-storage equipment which will allow transactions to be processed "on line," as opposed to the "batching" concept of sequential processing predominant in present equipment.

If the problem is analyzed in relation to this time dimension, some order begins to emerge from chaos. At the present time, most business-oriented computers can maintain a series of reports which approximate the information to which the auditor was accustomed under manual methods. This is especially true in operations limited to first-phase technological developments. The use of tape-oriented systems, however, may require extensive redesigning of the business information system in order to utilize the computer efficiently. In the second phase of development, it seems that the auditor should concentrate on the controls incorporated into the data-processing system. But there appears to be little need for an auditor to be able to program in order to perform an effective job of auditing. Under the conditions which exist today in most business firms his knowledge of the computer need only be minimal. The third phase of development is somewhat in the future, and although it is not as clear what direction auditing procedures should take, the problem is considered further in chapters vi and vii.

Unfortunately, the literature does not always reflect the views of the profession, for the more vocal members are not necessarily the spokesmen for the majority. It would probably be significant to test the attitudes of the profession as a whole, and to compare them with the thoughts expressed in the literature. A selective segment of the profession's outlook was considered even more pertinent, however, and was surveyed by distributing a questionnaire among accountants actually engaged in auditing business firms using business-oriented computers as an integral part of the data-processing system. This questionnaire is unique in that no such survey had previously been made successfully. (An earlier effort, several years ago, revealed chiefly that the auditing profession was not yet aware of the problems being investigated.) The remainder of chapter v discusses and evaluates the current attitudes of the public accounting profession as expressed in the responses to the questionnaires.

Chapter vi suggests possible solutions to the problems of auditing a computerized data-processing system. The primary reason for supplementing the control approach with other techniques is that the auditor, whenever possible, is obligated to give the client the maximum benefit from the time spent on the engagement, and with a minimum disruption of the client's normal accounting procedures. Currently, the auditor considers the computer as an obstacle to be overcome or circumvented in order to accomplish his objective. It would be highly desirable, if feasible, to turn the problem around—to view the computer as an aid in performing the audit more effectively and more efficiently. There are a number of problems in this approach, and the profession at the present time is highly skeptical of the success of this approach.

There are two possible ways to deal with the problem. One, relatively cruder, is to use the computer to audit the transactions of a business firm in the traditional sense. That is, the computer operations follow the same steps a junior accountant takes; comparison of the results of the computer run and the results previously obtained by the client's data-processing staff then suggests some conclusions as to the effectiveness of the data-processing operation. The alternative approach, still in its embryonic development, involves the additional step of making the decision, based upon results obtained from the computer run, as to the modifications which should take place in the audit program. For example, by building certain acceptable criteria into the audit program, the computer can generate as output some tentative conclusions regarding the system of internal control. This is illustrated in chapter vi.

Chapter vii discusses possible developments during the next decade. The public accounting practitioner is primarily concerned with the current problems of his clients; he typically gives little or no thought to the long-range objectives of auditing theory and practice. Although the Long Range Planning Committee of the American Institute of Certified Public Accountants functions notably in its arena, there is a need for more widespread consideration of developments which might occur and the consequent impact on the profession.

One of the ways in which this problem may be approached is to apply models like those developed in chapter vi to the problem of auditing a "real time" system where conceivably even the source documents might disappear. Although it is not possible to rely on the model alone to review the data-processing system, the controls built into the integrated system are an essential part of the audit program. And with a suitable balance between evaluation of the controls of the system and the use of a computer model, the auditor may still be able to conduct the examination in a manner which is not conceptually different from that of present-day practice. This conclusion provides a certain amount of assurance that the auditor will not have to become a data-processing expert in order to express an opinion on the financial statement of his clients.

This assurance should not, however, lull the auditing profession into a false sense of security. It is becoming increasingly important for the auditor to utilize the power of the computer whenever possible to assist him in his examination, and this procedure will become even more important as data-processing installations increase in size and complexity. Even now, although it is not necessary for an auditor to be a computer expert, it is necessary to include as a part of professional training an adequate study of electronic data-processing and its impact on business firms. It is the responsibility of the universities and colleges to initiate awareness of these developments in the student. It is the responsibility of the public accounting firm to continue this education and to adopt a policy of continual alertness to the developments which are occuring almost daily. This is not an either/or proposition. It is not a question of whether the universities or the public accounting firms provide the education and training. It must be a mutual effort, with sound, basic grounding started at the university level and then supplemented by the practical applications in the day-to-day operations of the public accounting firm.

This book is not concerned with the technical aspects of computer logic and programming as such. The text is relatively free of technical terms and programming details. The source programs for the computer models, written in FORTRAN, are provided in the Appendix for those who may be interested. Even in this case, however, the FORTRAN program has a relatively elementary logical structure. It could have been written by a practicing accountant with a minimal training in programming. If the auditing profession is to use the computer as suggested in chapter vi, it is desirable to use these computer models as prototypes in order to encourage a greater number of practitioners to examine the possibilities of this powerful tool. In chapter vi, as elsewhere, the basic aspects of the problem are emphasized, for it is with the broader aspects of the problem faced by the public accounting profession that this book is concerned. The technical problems of the computer are, by comparison, minor.

II

The Business Information System

Business firms in general, and public accounting firms as their consultants, have become increasingly cognizant of the role of the business information system in effective management, especially during the past
ten to fifteen years. This increasing awareness of the crucial role of
systems design is due to a number of underlying causes:

(1) The failure of traditional accounting systems to supply data
relevant to managerial decision making.

(2) The increasing emphasis on "real-time" reporting, as opposed
to receiving information after a significant time lag.

(3) The lack of a competent clerical staff for manually processing
data required by the more rigorous demands of an expanding business
information system.

(4) The accentuation of the struggle to keep data-processing costs
"realistic."

(5) The impact of the current literature on managerial decision
making.

The Lack of a Generally Accepted Theory

In searching for definitive theoretical statements about the ideal structure of a business information system, the lack of substantive content in
the approaches and arguments currently advanced by leaders of the
business community becomes more than apparent. The contributions of
the academic profession are also somewhat limited in this area. In other
words, there is no generally accepted theory of business information
systems.

The lack of a sound theoretical basis underlying systems design has
created a plethora of descriptive techniques and a number of pedestrian
descriptions of a business information system.[1] These seem to serve no

---

[1] See Norman N. Barish, *Systems Analysis for Effective Administration* (New
York: Funk & Wagnalls, 1951), chap. i; James D. Gallagher, *Management Infor-
mation Systems and the Computer,* American Management Association Research
Study No. 51 (New York: The Association, 1961); and Robert I. Dickey, ed., and
Accountants' Cost Handbook (2d ed.; New York: Ronald Press, 1960), chap. iv.

useful purpose in determining the conceptual framework which under-
lies systems design. Lacking a structured context, one might approach
the problem by observing the actual operations of business systems and
then attempt to establish some underlying principles of systems design.
But even if we assume that the almost insuperable problems of data
collection could be overcome, this approach would be inadequate. The
almost universal method of developing business systems has been a
matter of "adding on."[2] Except in a few rare instances, business information systems have emerged with something of a patchwork
design.[3]

The lack of integration and uniformity in business information systems is also evident in the relatively meager success of equipment manufacturers in designing packaged systems. Packaged systems are still subject to relatively high installation costs and the consequent extended
pay-out periods may force a negative recommendation as to the prac-
ticality of an electronic data-processing installation.[4]

The Objectives of a Business Information System

With business firms looking to their public accounting firms for assistance and advice on systems design, it becomes mandatory for management services people to have some "ideal" or "norm" toward which to
strive in developing business information systems. There are today fewer
constraints than formerly in developing practical systems; technological
developments in the sixties have rapidly expanded the possibilities for
improved system design. But the mere existence of sophisticated hardware does not solve the problem.

Review of the ideas expressed by various disciplines is a necessary
first step towards intelligent solutions, and the objectives of a business
information system serve as a useful frame of reference for this review:
(1) to provide business firms with information required for managerial
decision making; (2) to provide the necessary information for the development of general purpose financial statements; (3) to provide an
efficient system of internal control. The concept of a business information system is broader than that of an accounting system. It is not
limited merely to accounting information. A good information system
attempts to provide management with all relevant information, whether

---

[2] M. E. Salveson, "Computers in the Design of Business Organizations," *Electronics in Action,* American Management Association Special Report No. 22 (New
York: The Association, 1957), pp. 129-149.

[3] Gallagher, *op. cit.,* Appendixes A and B.

[4] See summary of answers to questionnaire in Appendix B.

the quantitative data be monetary or statistical, or even when qualitative variables need to be considered.

In order to achieve its goals, the design of a business information system must include consideration of inputs and outputs as well as a transformation mechanism to convert inputs into relevant and useful outputs. It is assumed that initially the objectives of the system are determined by management, but we also need some flexibility in order to consider possible alternatives and a means of reconciling conflicting procedures within the system itself.

THE CONTRIBUTION OF ECONOMIC THEORY

The concept of a business firm as visualized by the neo-classical economists in the world of perfect competition considers the firm as a system. In the words of Kenneth Boulding:

A firm may be defined as an institution which buys things, transforms them in some way, and then sells them with the purpose of making a profit. The things a firm buys we shall call "inputs." The things it sells we shall call "outputs." . . . A business, therefore, is a process whereby certain inputs, valued in dollars in some way, are transformed into outputs, also valued in dollars in some way.[5]

All the essential elements of a system are included in this definition. The production function is the transformation mechanism for the conversion of inputs into output, and, in view of the goal of the firm as postulated in the theory of perfect competition, points on the production surface will be selected which are optimal with respect to the criterion function. These by definition become the most "efficient" points of operation for the business firm; the business system can be said to be stable, and an equilibrium position is reached which is unique to the particular firm.

The "black box" in the system is the transformation mechanism. This mechanism is assumed to exist, but is not explicitly handled in neo-classical economics. Joel Dean recognized this shortcoming in the theory of the firm and wrote *Managerial Economics* in order

to show how economic analysis can be used in formulating business policies. It is therefore a departure from the main stream of economic writings on the theory of the firm, much of which is too simple in its assumptions and too complicated in its logical development to be managerially useful. The big gap between the problems of logic that intrigue economic theorists

---

[5] Kenneth E. Boulding, *Economic Analysis* (3d ed.; New York: Harper & Brothers, 1955), pp. 493-495.

and the problems of policy that plague practical management needs to be
bridged in order to give executives access to the practical contributions
that economic thinking can make to top-management policies.[6]

Spencer and Siegelman express a similar purpose: "Business economics
. . . may be defined as the integration of economic theory with business practice for the purpose of facilitating decision making and forward planning by management."[7]

The development of managerial economics resulted basically from
the dissatisfaction which existed with the underlying assumptions of
neo-classical theory. The pioneering works by Berle and Means and
R. A. Gordon greatly influenced the economic theorists. The manager,
it was demonstrated, is no longer the owner; the motivations which
were assumed in traditional economic theory were shown to be invalid
in the modern corporation with its characteristic separation between
ownership and management. While managerial economists were attempting to modify classical theory to bridge this gap, other disciplines
also became interested in the problem.

ORGANIZATION THEORY

Organization theory, often considered the domain of business administration, is more accurately a synthesis of many disciplines concerned
with the same problems: internal activities and the operation of the
business firm. Although it is difficult to characterize organization theory
from a single point of view, it may be said to be fundamentally concerned with attempting to understand the nature of the business process.
Game theory and decision theory, information theory and communication theory, small group theory and developments in motiva-
tional research—all can be focused on the central topic.[8] In developing
a concept of a business information system, it is crucial to explore the
pertinent contributions of organization theory, although recognizing
that current writings are merely the conceptual beginnings of what
may ultimately develop into a comprehensive theory of business organization.

One of the models helpful in the present context is contained in Herbert Simon's *Administrative Behavior*. This model of a business firm

---

[6] Joel Dean, *Managerial Economics* (Englewood Cliffs, N.J.: Prentice-Hall, 1951), p. vii.

[7] Louis Siegelman and Milton H. Spencer, *Managerial Economics* (Homewood, Ill.; Richard D. Irwin, 1959), Introduction to part i.

[8] Mason Haire, ed., *Modern Organization Theory* (New York: John Wiley & Sons, 1959), pp. 1-2.

with certain simplifying assumptions fits rather closely into the emerging concept of a business information system:

> In the pages of this book, the term organization refers to the complex pattern of communications and other relations in a group of human beings. This pattern provides to each member of the group much of the information, assumptions, goals, and attitudes that enter into his decisions, and provides him also with a set of stable and comprehensible exceptions as to what the other members of the group are doing and how they will react to what he says and does. The sociologist calls this pattern a "role system"; to most of us it is more familiarly known as an "organization."[9]

In Simon's model of organizations, ethical values are taken as the givens; the administrator seeks to adjust the organization by using the means at his disposal, including authority, communication, loyalties, and organizational identification. Simon visualizes communication as central to the existence of an organization: "Communication may be formally defined as any process whereby decisional premises are transmitted from one member of an organization to another. It is obvious that without communication there can be no organization, for there is no possibility then of the group influencing the behavior of the individual."[10]

Jacob Marschak also stresses the importance of communication in the development of "team theory": "The workings of an organization might be better understood if, instead of the usual 'organization chart,' one could have the description—if only very rough—of 'who does what in response to what information?' "[11] This statement paraphrases the essence of the task of the systems designer, who must measure the response in relation to a criterion function if he is to complete the necessary structure for systems design.

Rensis Likert in his recently published *New Patterns of Management* is critical of the present output of the business information system:

> It is difficult, if not impossible, to build and maintain a highly effective interaction-influence system without the guiding information provided by adequate measurements of the causal and intervening variables. It is hard to tell from the production, earnings, and cost data, for example, how well the overlapping group structure of an organization is function-

---

[9] Herbert A. Simon, *Administrative Behavior* (2d ed.; New York: Macmillan, 1958), introduction, p. xvi.

[10] *Ibid.*, p. 154.

[11] Jacob Marschak, "Efficient and Viable Organizational Forms," in Haire, *op. cit.*, p. 309.

ing and how adequate and accurate the communication processes are. Moreover, it is hard to tell from measures of cost and earnings whether particular attempts to improve any operations such as upward communication actually do so and which kinds of changes are bringing the greatest improvement. Measurements are needed which deal with all the important processes of an organization if a highly effective interaction-influence system is to be built and maintained.[12]

Likert proposes to alter the traditional information movement, which at present is principally an upward flow. He would direct the information to the work group by providing regular summary reports of the organization as a whole and of the functional subdivision of which the group is a part. Likert adds a note of caution, however, suggesting that systems designers should not overwhelm the members of the organization with a large amount of information dealing with a wide array of variables. The introduction of the new system should proceed gradually, allowing time for learning and assimilation by the members of the organization, and for their behavioral adjustment.

INFORMATION THEORY AND COMMUNICATION THEORY

One of the vital threads relating the contribution of organization theory to the notion of a business information system has been the role of information and communication within the systems concept. It may be well at this point to digress briefly, to examine the contribution of information theory and communication theory.

Information theory is primarily concerned with the technical aspects of the content of communication. It has developed largely on the momentum generated by the pioneering efforts of Norbert Weiner[13] and Claude E. Shannon.[14] As was pointed out by Warren Weaver in his portion of *The Mathematical Theory of Communication,* communication theory includes information theory as a necessary ingredient.[15]

There are in essence three levels at which the communication problem may be considered. One level is concerned with the accuracy of the communication (information theory). As used by Shannon, "information is a measure of one's freedom of choice when one selects a message." A second level is concerned with the precision by which the transmitted symbols convey the desired meaning (the semantic prob-

---

[12] Rensis Likert, *New Patterns of Management* (New York: McGraw-Hill, 1961), p. 192.

[13] Norbert Wiener, *Cybernetics* (New York: John Wiley & Sons, 1948).

[14] Claude E. Shannon and Warren Weaver, *The Mathematical Theory of Communication* (Urbana, Ill.: University of Illinois Press, 1959).

[15] *Ibid.,* p. 97.

lem). The third level is concerned with the observable results of the conduct of the recipient in reacting to the transmitted symbols (the comparison of desired objectives with the achieved results).

As used in the phrase "business information system," information is a broader concept; in fact, here the word implies all of the concepts included in the over-all definition of communication theory. Both the semantic and the effectiveness criteria are of crucial importance to a business information system. Indeed, the effectiveness of the communication is considered to be the central focus of the systems designer.

OPERATIONS RESEARCH AND THE BUSINESS INFORMATION SYSTEM

Operations research, as viewed in broad perspective, is also concerned with the problem of a business system. In fact, it has been asserted that the organization theory is a necessary foundation for the development of operations research. This is not universally true, however. There appear to be two basic, diametrically opposed philosophical approaches to operations research. The first point of view is stressed by Charles Hitch, as succinctly restated by C. West Churchman: "The development of an optimal plan for a larger organization is essentially the study of a set of 'suboptimal' problems which can realistically be solved, rather than the direct solution of the optimal over-all strategy."[16] This viewpoint is very close to the way in which the concept of a business information system has developed in industry today, which appears to imply that the "suboptimal" problems must be recognized and solved before the over-all strategy can be planned. But there is certainly ample evidence that sub-systems within a business system are not necessarily independent, and indeed, the opposing point of view stresses the over-all approach to operations research and to systems design. In essence this point of view holds that in order to optimize any segment of an organization, one must optimize the whole.

These opposing points of view cannot be completely reconciled, but there seems to be some meeting ground which may be helpful to a consideration of business information systems. The use of the word "business" connotes concentration on one particular business entity. Therefore, it seems desirable that the "whole" be considered as the business firm independent of any national or industry ties. But it also seems obvious that the attempt to break down the business information system—into subparts in which the accounting implications can be con-

---

[16] C. West Churchman, "Decision and Value Theory," in Russell L. Ackoff, ed., *Progress in Operations Research* (New York: John Wiley & Sons, 1961), p. 45.

sidered separately from the rest of the system—is not only undesirable and uneconomic, it may also lead to independent conclusions in which the over-all impact on the business information system might conceivably be adverse. For example, if considered as separate from managerial functions, the requirements of the accounting system may substantially alter the form and timing of reports submitted to other departments of the company. As a matter of fact, the exclusion of managerial accounting analysis from the regular accounting framework has in many cases created complications in the reporting relationships which have been extremely expensive and inefficient.

ESSENTIAL ELEMENTS OF A BUSINESS INFORMATION SYSTEM

It may be well at this point to note some of the important differences between business systems and other systems before attempting to outline the normative characteristics of a business information system. In the words of Malcolm W. Hoag:

The proper course for an operations researcher, I think, is to determine, first what the real problem is, and second, the appropriate system within which this problem must be considered if it is to be fruitfully solved. An alternative course is to establish first what the system to be studied is, and then to inquire about the problems of that system. This alternative course is the natural one for an administrator to take, for he is charged with looking after an organization whose boundaries will usually have been defined.[17]

Here, then, is a substantive difference between the problems faced by the designer of the business information system and those of an analyst faced with broader issues.

A useful contrast can also be made between a business information system and an engineering system. The literature of mechanical engineering observes that "All control has a common theoretical basis regardless of whether it is of a processing plant, telemetric receiver, or servo-operated rudder. . . . Regulation is control to a particular set value or following a given law."[18] The important point to note in connection with this definition is the absence of any uncontrolled or unpredictable variable. In the theory of system design as viewed from the engineering standpoint, the character of the environment can be esti-

---

[17] Malcolm W. Hoag, "What Is a System?" *Operations Research,* Vol. V (June, 1957).

[18] Ed Sinclair Smith, *Automatic Control Engineering* (New York, McGraw-Hill, 1944), p. 1.

mated after due allowance for noise in the system. The chief concern of the systems designer is to design the control mechanism in such a way that hunting is damped down and a stable system is created, or at least to contain the oscillation of the system within tolerable constraints.

On the other hand, the business system "is a particular combination of human service, material service, and equipment service acting on information to accomplish a goal."[19] The element of human service, which is not included in the engineering concept, is basic. Thus, in a business system the control loop may not be completely closed and the principle of damping oscillatory movements by employing negative feedback may not be applicable. The adjustment, which must be recognized by the designer of business systems, is the use of alternative courses of action depending on the interaction between the human and the physical components of the system.

Tentatively, then, the essential elements of a business information system may be summarized:

(1) A set of objectives for the business firm.

(2) A list of alternative courses of action by which these goals can be approximated.

(3) Efficiency measures by which these alternative courses of action can be assessed in terms of the organizational objectives.

(4) A policy, or set of policies, by which the manager can obtain or move toward the objectives of the business firm.

(5) A means of dividing the policy into functional subparts.

(6) A means of comparing actual operations against established "norms" in such a way that appropriate signals will be generated to indicate when the system is out of control.

(7) Adequate safeguards in the design so that there is proper separation between program formulation and information processing.

As was indicated earlier, for the systems designer the first four elements are considered to be given. His first concern after determining these factors is to attempt to subdivide the policy. If policy is viewed as that portion of potential behavior which is relevant to the accomplishment of the goals of the business firm as viewed by the manager, it becomes clear that the problem is really one of decentralization.

Point 5 requires that an organization, or at least the business information system of an organization, can be subdivided. Subdivision is neces-

---

[19] Ned Chapin, *An Introduction to Automatic Computers* (Princeton, N.J.: D. Van Nostrand Company, 1957), p. 50.

sary in order to utilize a suboptimizing technique. Subdivision requires that the separated part of the firm be able to perform optimally within the group; consequently, it is able to advance the over-all goals by furthering the subgoals assigned to it. Information processing that follows the organizational structure will, then, be able to satisfy the requirements of the system by establishing a set of subgoals, alternative actions within this limited area, and efficiency measurement techniques, thus providing the manager with recommendations which can be verified by relating the data to the over-all objectives of the organization.

The idea of data collection does not directly enter into the listing of the minimum essentials of the system outlined. Data collection has only a secondary role in the business information system; it is implied in point 6, which suggests that data are important only as a means to an end, rather than the more traditional view that data collection may be an end in itself—the point of view still conventionally adopted by accountants.

Point 6 is concerned with the distinction between programmed and nonprogrammed decisions. A business information system must have appropriate flexibility for allowing the intervention of human decision makers whenever the system exceeds its capacity to regulate itself. This particular problem is central to the design of business information systems and is explicitly handled in the conceptual model of a business information system discussed later.

Point 7 restates the problem faced by the public accountant in evaluating the system of internal control. One of the primary concerns of the accountant is safeguarding the assets under the custody of the business firm. The usual procedure is to separate physical control and accounting. The counterpart of this idea in business information systems is to separate responsibility for EDP system design or programming from the actual operation of the system.

Ideally, a computerized business information system is an integrated data-processing (IDP) system. Realization of this concept of an integrated data-processing system is considered to be the major objective of the system of the future. So far as can be determined at the present time, however, there are no completely integrated data-processing systems in operation. And it is not clear that current feasibility studies actually contemplate full integration.

A Possible Approach

In an attempt to structure the basic idea of a business information system, a conceptualization of an integrated data-processing model is

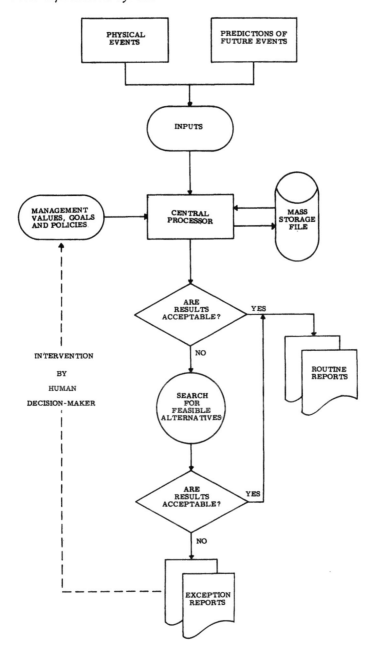

Fig. 1. Conceptualization of an integrated data processing system model.

outlined in figure 1. The model incorporates the basic notions of feed-back and "open loop" type flows characteristic of business systems. The starting point in any systems model is the physical activity or transaction which gives rise to some type of input into the system. Inputs must first be expressed in a standard language ("qualified") by means of some device, so that all data of a particular classification can be processed similarly. This requirement applies to a manual system as well as to a mechanized or electronic system. The central processor receives in-formation from three basic sources: (1) the standard-language input data, (2) the prescribed management policies or goals applicable to the particular phase of the operation, and (3) historical information or norms available from some type of mass-storage file. A comparison (whether simple or complex) is made between the prescribed policies together with their related norms, and the standardized input data. The functional format of the transformation mechanism requires that a decision be made as to whether the data are acceptable for transfer to routine progress reports, or whether the deviation is sufficiently signifi-cant to require further analysis.

If the data are acceptable, the operation of the system as it relates to that particular transaction is completed, and further inputs are proc-essed. If, however, the results are not acceptable, then the system pro-ceeds with further analysis seeking to determine some alternative solu-tion. After adjustment, the input data are again compared with the management policies and a decision is again made as to whether the data are acceptable. If the results are now acceptable, a so-called modified report becomes the output of the system, notifying the man-ager that the system, although substantially self-correcting, has, through a process of learning, modified the subgoals, and this information is supplied to management so that the current effective policy is known.

The operation of this particular phase of the system is essentially the use of feedback controlling the performance of the system through the means of a closed loop. A simple example may help to clarify this mechanism: Production goals, marketing goals, and financial con-straints are variously interdependent. If the criteria for the production schedule are established by using an inventory model, inputs for a given period might indicate significant deviations from the required norms. An adjustment of production subgoals may therefore be re-quired in conjunction with changes in the marketing or financial constraints. The inputs would then be compared with the adjusted production subgoal in order to determine the significance of whatever deviation still exists after production policy has been modified.[20] If results cannot be reconciled, the business information system has recourse to using the exception report technique to inform the manager.

This latter alternative incorporates the notion of an open-loop control with the previously discussed notion of a closed-loop system incorporating negative feedback. The system is self-contained, unless the deviations exceed the capacity of the system to adjust. Then the loop is breached and the manager has to step in and take whatever corrective measures seem to be indicated by the data furnished in the exception report.

The distinction made in this model between programmed decisions and nonprogrammed decisions is similar to the distinction made by Simon:

Decisions are nonprogrammed to the extent that they are novel, unstructured, and consequential. There is no cut-and-dried method for handling the problem because it hasn't arisen before, or because its precise nature and structure are elusive or complex, or because it is so important that it deserves a custom-tailored treatment.[21]

Simon goes on to point out that the current advances in heuristic programming techniques may herald the day when nonprogrammed decisions can be solved by computer programs. A great deal of work is, in fact, being done in this area today. For the purpose of this study, however, it need only be noted that the conceptual model is sufficiently flexible to incorporate heuristic programming techniques whenever it becomes feasible to do so. The logical structure of the EDP business information system does not change as a result of these innovations in programming techniques.

PROPOSED STANDARDS FOR BUSINESS INFORMATION SYSTEMS

A number of criteria merit consideration for guiding systems designers in the development of an EDP business information system model:

(1) The model must include more than a description of how a business system behaves; it must also include a normative element indicat-

[20] F. E. Balderston, "Optimal and Feasible Choices in Organizations Having Multiple Goals," Management Sciences Nucleus, Institute of Industrial Relations, University of California, Working Paper No. 12 (Berkeley, Calif.: The Institute, Feb., 1960).

[21] Herbert A. Simon, *The New Science of Management Decision* (New York: Harper & Brothers, 1960), p. 6.

ing how business men ought to behave. The availability of alternative courses of action must be an integral part of the system. This implies the use of weighting in assigning the consequences of adopting alternative courses of action. The implication is clear that the systems designer has the burden of determining the kind of data which management will need to evaluate alternative action choices.

(2) The model must recognize feedback as an essential in meeting the problem of adapting behavior to changing stimuli—either in the parameters of the model or in goal conflicts within the system. In the ordinary case the accountant records deviations from the norm but continues to report as if they had no effect upon the system itself; change is considered, in effect, external to the system. An efficient information system must not only record these variations but must allow for corrective action within the system itself or, as a last resort, provide a communication channel with the manager. (It is significant that traditional system design has not provided for consideration of normative behavior or for negative feedback. Computers are not essential to the implementation of these ideas, but they do allow a greater flexibility in system design.)

(3) The requirements set forth by communication theory must be fulfilled by the model. The three criteria of communication systems— the engineering criterion, the semantic criterion, and the effectiveness criterion—must be used to assess the efficiency of the communication network incorporated in the business information system model.

(4) Storage and efficient retrieval of data are of primary importance to the systems designer. In communication theory, the problem of information retrieval is not basic. It is central to business systems, however. The generation and storage of data without efficient access robs the system of its full potential. Current developments in information retrieval theory and mass-storage devices have changed the traditional look-up problems of the accountant. Thus, the designer must consider the economics of rapid data retrieval and the relative importance of maintaining a permanent record of transactions.

(5) The implementation phase of the business information system model is vital to its successful utilization. The cost of operation of the system must, in the last analysis, be balanced against the effectiveness of the system. It is only in connection with this last point that it is possible to assess fully the impact of current developments in computer technology.

III

The Development Of The Business-Oriented Computer

This chapter traces the relevant historical developments of the business-oriented computer. Technical aspects of computers are mentioned only briefly and insofar as they affect the operation EDP business information system. Contrary to the opinion shared by many people, discussion of the "hardware"[1] is useful. The basic ideas utilized in computer design are neither novel nor startling in the light of developments which have occurred during the last one hundred and twenty-five years, but they serve as guidelines for the development of current business information systems. Furthermore, placing the computer in historical perspective suggests possible future developments.

Definition of a Business-Oriented Computer

Although computer terminology is gradually standardizing, confusion still exists regarding many of the terms in current use. Therefore, it is desirable to delimit at the outset the areas which are to be considered by defining, at least tentatively, what is meant by the business-oriented computer. Computer manufacturers refer to "electronic computers," by which term they intend to convey a picture of a "stored-program"[2] machine operating on the digital principle[3] and able to perform rapidly logical and arithmetic operations through the use of electronic circuits.

---

[1] "Hardware" has become the accepted term for the electronic components which comprise a data-processing system. "Software" comprises the computer programs supplied by the manufacturer to assist in the implementation and operation of the computer components.

[2] "Stored program" refers to the list of instructions read into the memory of the electronic computer. The concept of the stored program is the fundamental idea associated with the electronic computer, distinguishing it from other types of mechanized equipment.

[3] As opposed to an analogue computer. (See below, fn. 5.)

Others, too, often refer to this class of equipment as electronic computers.[4]

Chapin uses the term "automatic computer," defining the equipment as "a high-speed, automatic, electronic, digital data-processing machine."[5] There seems to be a growing tendency to use this term, which emphasizes the functional, rather than the energy, characteristics of computers: having once been given a complete set of instructions, they proceed to process data automatically—without further human intervention. Although the computer certainly has this ability, there is an unfortunate connotation in the word "automatic" of operation without human guidance. Since automatic operations occur only after a series of comprehensive instructions have been provided by the systems designer, programmer, and console operator, the term can be misleading to persons not specializing in the field, and is therefore avoided in this discussion.

Hartree distinguishes between "instruments" and "machines." A "machine" can handle only numbers expressed in digital form to a finite number of significant figures; it cannot deal with continuous variables or continuous processes as such, and, in particular, when a machine is used, integration has to be replaced by summation over a finite number of finite intervals.[6] Although Hartree's classification distinguishes only between digital and analogue machines, other writers refer to a particular class of digital computers. The concept which seems to describe most accurately the type of equipment which is discussed in this chapter is "stored-program digital computer."

The stored program characteristic is the distinguishing feature by means of which operating instructions are stored in the same way and the same place as the data that are to be processed. Instructions stored in the computer memory can be manipulated exactly as if they were data. "Computer," denoting calculating ability, completes the concept.

The stored-program digital computer was developed through a series of steps; it was long treated primarily as a mathematical and scientific tool. Indeed, this is understandable, for the computer[7] developed in response to the need of scientists, engineers, and mathematicians, rather than the demands of the business community. But its origins have had

---

[4] See, for example, Harold Borko, ed., *Computer Applications in the Behavioral Sciences* (Englewood Cliffs, N.J.: Prentice-Hall, 1962), pp. 50-51.

[5] Ned Chapin, *An Introduction to Automatic Computers* (Princeton, N.J.: D. Van Nostrand Company, 1957), p. 4.

[6] Douglas R. Hartree, *Calculating Instruments and Machines* (Urbana, Ill.: University of Illinois Press, 1949), p. 2.

[7] For brevity, the "stored-program digital computer" is referred to simply as "computer."

prejudicial consequences; as was mentioned earlier, there has been more emphasis on the logical structure and internal speeds of the machine than on the input-output devices. By and large, scientific and technical problems require very little input, and typically produce a small number of decision rules or a single number as output. As Borko observes, the computer has come to be more than a research device; it is a production tool; but this view tends to overlook the persisting tremendous disparity between the speeds of the input-output devices and the internal speeds of the central processing unit. If the computer is to be successfully used as a production tool, much additional study must be given to this problem. Data processing[8] for business applications requires an entirely different perspective from that originally contemplated by the people responsible for the major developments in computer technology. As has already been indicated, computers which are modified or adapted for business data-processing systems are widely referred to as business-oriented computers, a practice to which this study will conform.

DEVELOPMENTS PRIOR TO 1800

The earliest development in digital computers was literally digital computing—counting on the fingers. This "technology" made its first known advance in the Near East several thousand years before Christ by using notched sticks or knotted strings to record quantitative information. The Chinese developed a machine called the abacus, *ca.* 3,000 B.C., which is still used today in the Orient. It uses the position of beads for numerical representation. Both Borko and Chapin (more comprehensively) list a chronology of early computing developments. Both authors consider the abacus, Napier's Bones, Pascal's adding machine, and Leibnitz's stepped cylinder as significant milestones in the development of digital computers.

Unfortunately, technological developments did not keep pace with the theoretical ideas of the advanced thinkers who created early computers. Neither Leibnitz nor Pascal was able to develop a reliable computing device. There is some evidence from a recent archeological discovery that the Greeks in 30 B.C. had used the idea of stepped cylinders to develop astronomical tables; the evidence is rather meager, but these may have been the first working models of a true digital computer.[9]

---

[8] Data processing in this, its broadest meaning, refers to the whole range of operations from input of data to output of results.

[9] Derek Price and John De Solla, *Science Since Babylon* (New Haven, Conn.: Yale University Press, 1961).

Table 1 contains the historically significant dates in the development of the business-oriented computer.

TABLE 1

HISTORY OF THE BUSINESS-ORIENTED COMPUTER[a]

Year	Person or company responsible	Designation	Description
3000 B.C.		Abacus	Calculating device with beads
30 B.C.		Digital machine	Greek innovation for astronomical calculations
1617	Napier	Napier's Bones	Multiplication device
1642	Pascal	Calculating machine	First calculating machine
1672	Leibnitz	Multiplication machine	Improvement on Pascal's machine using stepped cylinder
1842	Babbage	Difference engine	Machine for calculating tables by means of differences
1850	Babbage	Analytical engine	Theoretical design for a stored program digital computer
1890	Hollerith	Punched cards	Development of machinery for processing census data
1944	Aiken	Mark I	First general purpose computer
1946	Eckert & Mauchly	ENIAC	First use of electronic circuitry in computers
1951	Mauchly, Eckert, & von Neumann	EDVAC	Use of binary mode and internal memory
1951	Remington-Rand	UNIVAC-1	First commercially available computer
1953	M.I.T.	Whirlwind I	First use of magnetic core memory
1954	I.B.M.	650	First computer to gain wide market acceptance
1957	I.B.M.	RAMAC 305	Introduced concept of high-speed access to data stored randomly
1960	I.B.M.	1401	First business-oriented computer
1961	Minneapolis-Honeywell	400	Competitor to 1401
1961	R.C.A.	301	Competitor to 1401
1961	G.E.	225	Competitor to 1401
1962	N.C.R.	315	Introduction of mass-storage device called CRAM
1962	Burroughs	B 260, 270, 280	Competitor to 1401
1963	I.B.M.	1440	New concept in mass-storage devices

[a] Larger computers such as the B 5000, IBM 7090-94, RCA 601, Control Data 1604, and others have been omitted from this chronology although they may be used for business data processing as well as for scientific and research-oriented applications.

Initial modern developments in the concept of the computer are usually associated with the name of Charles Babbage. There is some question, as Chapin indicates, whether Babbage borrowed his basic idea for a so-called Difference Engine from earlier ideas developed by Muller. Babbage's own claim was that

One evening I was sitting in the rooms of the Analytical Society, at Cambridge, my head leaning forward on the Table in a kind of dreamy mood, with a Table of Logarithms lying open before me. Another member, coming into the room, and seeing me half asleep, called out, "Well, Babbage, what are you dreaming about?" to which I replied, "I am thinking that all these Tables (pointing to the logarithms) might be calculated by machinery."[10]

This happened in either 1812 or 1813. The advantages of using the method of differences for calculating tables are readily apparent, and a machine based on this method need not be particularly versatile, for all such tables can be calculated by one uniform process. Such a process does not require any arithmetic concept more sophisticated than that of addition.

In 1823, the Chancellor of the Exchequer lent his support to Babbage's project because, "as mathematical Tables were peculiarly valuable for nautical purposes, it was deemed a fit object of encouragement by the Government." Although the Lords of the Treasury advanced £1,500 for the construction of the Difference Engine, by 1827 these funds and at least an additional £3,000 of Babbage's personal funds were exhausted. In 1829, the government allotted an additional grant of £1,500. By 1837 Babbage had spent at least £17,000 and fourteen years on a project originally scheduled to take two to three years and budgeted for £3,000. After considerable correspondence and delay, the work was finally suspended on November 4, 1842, on the recommendation of Sir Robert Peel and Chancellor of the Exchequer Goulburn. Only a portion of the Difference Engine was ever constructed; it now is located in the Science Museum of London.

Babbage was not idle during the succeeding years. His inventive genius concentrated on a more advanced design, which he referred to as the Analytical Engine. Combining the ideas of analytical formulae with the Jacquard loom principle, whereby a set of punched-hole pasteboard cards inserted into the machine guides the pattern of its weaving, Babbage conceived of the Analytical Engine as follows:

---

[10] Charles Babbage, *Passages from the Life of a Philosopher* (London: Longman, Roberts & Green, 1864), p. 42.

The Analytical Engine consists of two parts:—1st. The store in which all the variables to be operated upon, as well as those quantities which have arisen from the result of other operations, are placed. 2nd. The mill into which the quantities about to be operated upon are always brought.

. . . There are therefore two sets of cards, the first to direct the nature of the operations to be performed—these are called operation cards; the other to direct the particular variables on which those cards are required to operate—these latter are called variable cards.[11]

Babbage's Analytical Engine ideas have a familiar ring to those acquainted with the basic logic of the computer. But, unfortunately for posterity, the Analytical Engine was never built. Babbage's plea to Sir Robert Peel for a re-hearing on the decision to abandon the Difference Engine was originally to be accompanied by a report discussing the advantages to be gained from starting construction of the Analytical Engine. Due to the state of Sir Robert's knowledge, the report was never presented. The interview was completely unsatisfactory.

The ingenuity and labors expended on the Analytical Engine have never been fully appreciated. Babbage was far ahead of his time. The obstacles to successful development of a computer in 1850 were in line with the times: the shortsightedness of the English government and the lack of technical skill able to give substance to his inventive genius. His youngest son, Henry P. Babbage, has preserved his father's basic ideas in *Babbage's Calculating Engines*.[12]

HERMAN HOLLERITH AND THE PUNCHED CARD

The impetus for Babbage's work came from the need for improvements in traditional means of calculating nautical, astronomical, and mathematical tables. The next significant development arose from the need to process large quantities of data for the United States Census of 1890. The punched card concept was a natural solution to this problem. A significant difference between the concept of the Analytical Engine and the punched card concept is that the punched card does not itself control the course of computation. In a sense, it is a step backward from Babbage's notion of using cards both to control the operation of the machine and to establish the quantitative valuation of the data.

The problem of census calculations, however, dictated a solution in which programming was not of the essence. In 1890 Herman Hollerith

---

[11] *Ibid.*, pp. 118-119.

[12] Henry P. Babbage, *Babbage's Calculating Engines, Being a Collection of Papers Relating to Them, Their History, and Construction* (London: E. and F. N. Spon, 1889).

developed the idea of state (hole vs. no hole) to represent in symbolic form the answers to mutually exclusive alternative categories. Although his machine—the sorter—was not oriented directly to business-type problems, it marked an important milestone in the handling of large quantities of input data. International Business Machines, Remington-Rand, and Underwood, among others, recognized the potentialities of this idea and subsequently developed punched card systems for business installations.

HOWARD AIKEN, I.B.M., AND THE MARK I

After Hollerith, nothing of significance developed for some time in either the scientific or business-oriented applications of data processing. The next significant development in the history of computers began when Professor Howard Aiken of Harvard University, in a discussion with George C. Chase on April 22, 1937, stated that some branches of science had reached a barrier which could not be passed until means could be found which would solve mathematical problems too large to be undertaken with the then-known computer equipment. During the seven years from 1937 to 1944, Aiken and International Business Machines engaged in a joint venture in the Computation Laboratory at Harvard. From this work emerged the Mark I I.B.M. Automatic Sequence-Controlled Calculator.[13]

The physical configuration of the machine was enormous, measuring 50 by 8 by 2 feet. But the components were amazingly simple, making use of switches, relays, buttons, and cam contacts. Information could be fed into the machine by regular punched cards, by hand-set dial switches, or by punched paper tape. The output could be handled in any one of three ways: by punching cards with a regular card punch built into the machine, by typing on paper sheets with electric typewriters, or by punching paper tape 24 holes wide (the same kind used for input). Programming instructions were handled by switch settings, use of buttons, plugboard wiring, or punched paper tape.

Writing about this machine in 1949, Berkeley observed:

In many respects, this machine is efficient and well-balanced. Its reading and writing speed is close to its calculating speed. We can punch or print a result on the average for every 10 additions or 1½ multiplications. The memory of 72 numbers in the machine is extremely useful; a smaller memory is a serious limitation on the achievements of a computing machine.

---

[13] Edmund C. Berkeley, *Giant Brains, or Machines That Think* (New York: John Wiley & Sons, 1949), p. 89.

. . . It has computed and tabulated Bessel functions, definite integrals, etc. It can solve differential equations and many other problems in mathematics, physics, and engineering.[14]

Despite its relatively slow time (3/10 of a second) for adding, subtracting, transferring, or clearing numbers, this machine represents the first of the general-purpose computers. Almost all discussions of this and succeeding computers, however, emphasize their scientific and mathematical possibilities.[15]

The ENIAC and the EDVAC

The Ordnance Department of the U.S. Army had long been concerned with the computational aspects of ballistics problems, and during World War II the problem became acute. The Electronic Numerical Integrator and Calculator (ENIAC), conceived at the Moore School of Electrical Engineering of the University of Pennsylvania as a possible solution to this problem, was completed in February, 1946, under the direction of Dr. J. W. Mauchly and Dr. J. P. Eckert. The two principal innovations which ENIAC introduced were the utilization of electronic tubes for calculating (as opposed to electro-mechanical switches and relays) and a significant increase in internal speed to approximately 5,000 additions a second.

ENIAC was an important step in the development of computers, but there were severe limitations to its usefulness. One of the most serious was the problem of built-in reliability and how reliability could be checked. Berkeley suggested three methods of checking reliability, none of which he deemed completely satisfactory:

1. Mathematical, if and when available, and this will be seldom.
2. Running the problem a second time, and this will, at most, prove consistency.
3. Deliberate testing of small parts of the problem which is very useful and is standard practice but leads only to a probability that the final results are correct.[16]

The internal reliability of the computer, which is all but taken for granted today, posed a serious problem to all early designers of comput-

---

[14] *Ibid.*, p. 111.

[15] For example: ". . . Mark I was conceived as a scientific table maker of high precision." Robert V. D. Campbell, "Evolution of Automatic Computation," in *Proceedings of the Association for Computing Machinery* (Pittsburgh: Richard Rimbach Associates, 1952), p. 1.

[16] Berkeley, *op. cit.*, p. 126.

ing machinery. Bell Telephone Laboratories' general-purpose relay computer was probably the best mechanical brain made up to the end of 1947—best, that is, in regard to the two important factors of reliability and versatility. The checking principle was a simple one. The machine was programmed to insure that exactly two out of seven relays are energized for each decimal digit (each decimal digit has seven relays). If fewer than two, or more than two relays are energized in a particular operation, the machine stops until the trouble is located. This arrangement insured that the machine would not execute the next instruction unless the previous instruction met the parity test. The probability of a mistake has been calculated to be approximately 0.000000001 per cent. According to a statement by Franz L. Alt, director of the Computing Laboratory at the Ballistic Research Laboratories, in December, 1947, "the Bell machine had not given a single wrong result in eight months of operation, except when operators interfered with its normal running."

The other significant limitation on the ENIAC was the lack of an adequate internal memory. In the ENIAC, the "accumulators" provide the only form of storage. Although there are two accumulators, each serving as both adding and storage units (as do the storage registers in the Harvard Mark I Calculator), their independence precludes the use of one for storage of output from the other, without human intervention. Thus, storage of output of arithmetical processes is limited to each operation series. In effect, then, the readmission to the accumulator of the output of a former operation is not possible by retrieval from storage, but requires its being introduced as input again.

The major disadvantages of the ENIAC were recognized even before the computer was fully operational. The Electronic Discrete Variable Automatic Computer (EDVAC) was designed to overcome ENIAC's deficiencies. It was not fully operative until April, 1952, due primarily to the large number of engineering and personnel changes that were made during the construction period. The EDVAC made at least four significant improvements over the ENIAC: (1) use of the binary number system, and the conversion from decimal to binary language accomplished by the internal circuitry of the machine; (2) use of duplicate circuitry for check purposes; (3) use of acoustic delay lines, in which data are stored in the form of trains of acoustic pulses; (4) storage of the program in the internal memory of the computers.

The group which developed EDVAC at the Moore School of Electrical Engineering included, in addition to the original designers of the ENIAC, John von Neumann, A. W. Burks, and H. H. Goldstine. These three men continued their work at the Institute for Advanced Study,

Princeton, New Jersey. Their efforts there led to development of the IAS computer, which features the use of the binary system, the parallel arithmetic mode, the one-address command structure, and a capable selection of commands. The command features of this machine, its highly superior speed (from about two to better than ten times faster than EDVAC), and its fairly straightforward circuitry have made it very popular. In fact, the Princeton IAS computer can be considered as the forerunner of the most popular family of computers.

Another significant advance occurred at the Massachusetts Institute of Technology in 1953, with the development of the Whirlwind I computer. Its principal contribution was the use of small ferrite cores for storing binary digits. With a capacity of 1,024 words, each consisting of 16 binary digits, it provided access to any number in internal storage in only one microsecond, a tremendous increase in speed.

DEVELOPMENT OF LATER PROTOTYPES

Eckert and Mauchly, designers of ENIAC, had formed their own company, Electronic Control Company, which in the late forties decided to attempt to design an automatic computer that would be effective both in business applications and in scientific and technical applications. After a merger in 1949 with Remington-Rand (now Remington Rand Division of the Sperry Rand Corporation), the work continued, resulting in production of the UNIVAC-I (Universal Automatic Computer), which first became operational in April, 1951, and commercially available in October, 1951. The public became acquainted with UNIVAC through its predictions made on television on election day, 1952.

The UNIVAC was the first computer to incorporate the best features of computers developed earlier. Designed explicitly as a prototype which could be marketed successfully, it adopted the acoustic delay-line internal memory from the EDVAC, the one-address command structure from the IAS, and magnetic tape for the input-output medium from the Harvard Mark II. UNIVAC-I used acoustic delay-line circuitry only, however; after magnetic core storage was developed in 1953, the UNIVAC-II adopted this technology, too, and provided a larger memory capacity.

In other respects, too, the period following the introduction of the UNIVAC-I in the closing months of 1951 brought notable developments, perhaps more important in an educational than in a technological sense, and certainly in the structure of the computer industry. A number of small companies sprang up in the early fifties, and just as quickly were merged into the larger firms of the industry. For example, Electronic Computer Corporation merged into the Underwood Corporation as the Elecom Division; the Physical Research Corporation merged into Marchant Calculating Machine Company as the Research Division; the Computer Research Corporation merged into the National Cash Register Company as the Electronics Division. One of the later starters in the field, International Business Machines, did not begin serious research in the computer field until after the start of the Korean War in 1950.

TABLE 2
COMPARATIVE COMPUTER CENSUS

Computer	In use 12/51 (1)	In use 12/56 (1)	In use 3/61 (2)	On order 3/61 (2)	In use 7/62 (3)	In use 1/63 (4)	On order 1/63 (4)
IBM 650		566	1350	25	967	620	0
IBM RAMAC			375	175	787	630	0
IBM 1401			75	4000	2585	6100	1900
IBM 7040-44						24	83
UNIVAC I, II	1	39	74	1	65	44	0
UNIVAC III			0	35	0	31	98
UNIVAC SS 80/90			207	255	518	390	15
UNIVAC 1004						460	1820
DATATRON 205/220		56	159	12	55	97	0
B 260, 270, 280					15	121	82
B 5000						11	22
RCA 301			0	65	107	335	205
RCA 501			50	60	80	68	11
GE 210			23	28	50	79	4
GE 225			5	38	55	(a)	38
NCR/GE 304			40	15	29	29	0
NCR 315					7	110	135
NCR 390			5	150	160	422	275
H-800			12	50	38	55	8
H-400			0	(a)	13	66	40
MONROBOT XI			109	105	265	280	209

SOURCES: (1) Chapin, 1957, p. 239; (2) *Data Processing*, April, 1961, pp. 32-33; (3) *Datamation*, August, 1962, p. 61; (4) *Computers and Automation*, December, 1963, pp. 56-57.
a Not reported.

Between the end of 1951 and the end of 1955, a significant increase occurred in the number of computers in use. In December, 1951, only one computer was in use (a UNIVAC-I). By December, 1955, there were 184 IBM-650's, 26 UNIVAC-I's, 20 DATATRONS, 20 NCR-102's, and 56 other computers principally manufactured by IBM and

Sperry Rand. (Table 2 offers a census of computers in use in the early 1960's.) These numbers represent both scientific and business-oriented installations and one can only speculate about the distribution between these two types. Regarding business-oriented applications, Chapin considers this period as one of selective, nascent advance: "On the basis of what was learned, a few companies early elected to pioneer in the application in business of the automatic computer. These pioneer installations of 1954 and 1955 were closely watched, and were soon followed by other installations."[17]

The important point is that the experience of business firms in formulating ideas for business-oriented data-processing systems dates only from approximately 1955. The business community in general, and accountants and data-processing managers in particular, have done a phenomenal job in a relatively short span of time. Nevertheless, after a decade of growth a relatively untapped area remains which must be studied closely in order to obtain maximum utilization from this tremendous technological breakthrough. The primary problem area involves the relationship between the business information system and the computer. The importance of this relationship has been noted almost since the introduction of the computer into business. For example, speaking at the Third Annual Electronic Conference of the American Manufacturers' Association in New York City in February, 1957, Melvin E. Salveson, consultant in operations research and synthesis, General Electric Company, observed:

Because of the "wholeness" of a business organization, a change in one of its parts can (and often does) lead to other related changes in many other parts of the organization—that is, to a new design of the organization. . . . The electronic computer is an innovation as fundamental to the design of many business as the jet engine has been to the design of aircraft, or as digital control of machine tools is to manufacturing.

Similarities of Electronic Equipment

In order to understand the problems currently being encountered by public accounting practitioners, it is necessary to have at least a basic understanding of the type of computer hardware which is presently available. Although there are more than a dozen manufacturers in the field, it would serve no useful purpose to discuss each computer in detail. Table 3 provides a brief review of the characteristics of the most popular business-oriented computers. Only eight manufacturers are rep-

---

[17] Chapin, *op. cit.*, p. 2.

resented in this table, and in many cases only one or two computers for each manufacturer have been listed. Typically, manufacturers classify computers by numerical designations; in each series, the difference in various models is chiefly a matter of memory capacity and speed of operating cycles rather than of any structural or technological innovation in the input-output equipment. It has already been noted that the main problem in business-oriented computers seems to be the disparity between input-output characteristics and the speeds of the central processing unit; hence the variations within a series need not be elaborated here.

The basic functions of all computers can be separated into two general areas: the ability to add (and by extension to subtract, multiply, and divide) and the ability to perform elementary logical operations. The typical job assigned to a computer within a data-processing department of a business firm is concerned with both of these functions, and usually the logical decisions required are indeed at a very elementary level. Generally speaking, relatively small internal memories and rather limited logical capacity can satisfy the conventional business data-processing requirements. The locus of the limiting factors lies in the peripheral equipment, not in the central processor. The central processor can probably be considered to be relatively stable insofar as future technical developments are concerned. This is not to say that further technical developments in the central processor will not be important, but that they are less important to the business community than to the scientific community.

The first computer designed specifically for business applications was the IBM 1401, which was announced in the fall of 1959. In the press release announcing this computer, IBM President Thomas J. Watson, Jr., made the following statement:

In my judgment, IBM's principal contribution to the punched card field during 1959 was the introduction of the 1401 Data Processing System. The 1401 gives smaller businesses many features that were formerly associated only with much larger and substantially more expensive equipment. Among these features are: magnetic core storage, magnetic tape input and output, and higher speeds in card reading, card punching and printing.

Just as important, the 1401 serves as an economical bridge between punched card systems and EDP. Thus smaller growing businesses, as their needs increase, can make an easy transition into full scale electronic processing.

Other manufacturers followed with computers designed around this same idea. It is interesting to note that Watson's emphasis is on the

TABLE 3

TYPICAL BUSINESS-ORIENTED COMPUTERS[a]

Manufacturer	Computer	Input characteristics (Punched cards/min.)	(Paper tape charac./sec.)
International Business Machines	IBM 7044	250	500
Sperry Rand Corporation	UNIVAC III	700	500
Minneapolis-Honeywell	H-800	800	1000
Burroughs Corporation	B-5000	800	1000
Radio Corporation of America	RCA-501	600	1000
General Electric	GE-210	1500	200
Minneapolis-Honeywell	H-400	800	1000
National Cash Register	NCR-315	2000	1000
Sperry Rand Corporation	UNIVAC SS 80/90	600	500
General Electric	GE-225	1500	1000
Burroughs Corporation	B 260, 270, 280	800	1000
International Business Machines	IBM 1401	800	500
Radio Corporation of America	RCA-301	800	1000
National Cash Register	NCR 390	15	400
Sperry Rand Corporation	UNIVAC 1004	300	none
Monroe Calculating Machines	MONROBOT XI	15	20

characteristics of the input-output equipment rather than on the capabilities of the central processing unit. Reliable estimates indicate that roughly three-fourths of the business-oriented computer systems in operation today are based on this design principle—relatively small internal storage, limited logical capabilities, and relatively high-speed input-output devices.

Because of the tremendous investment in feasibility studies as well as the extremely costly implementation period, there appears to be a reluctance among computer users to make drastic revisions of computer systems. Given the economics of changeover and the apparent stability of the central processor for accounting and other business-type applications, auditors appear destined to encounter this type of computer in clients' offices more than any other configuration, at least for the next several years.

This is an unfortunate prospect. For one thing, it allows auditors to continue using conventional auditing methods, for the so-called batch-controlled systems require print-outs not unlike those of manual or punched card systems, thus strengthening the conviction that computer systems do not basically change auditing procedures and techniques. Moreover, the relative inflexibility of these systems tends to inhibit development of integrated systems design concepts. And since these systems lend themselves to programming in assembly-type lan-

TABLE 3
TYPICAL BUSINESS-ORIENTED COMPUTER[a]

Output characteristics (Punched cards/min.)	(Printer lines/min.)	Magnetic tape Read/Write Characters /sec.	Random Access Equipment Available	Buf- fered System	Compilers FOR- TRAN	COBOL	Average Monthly Rental ($ooo)
125	1100	90000	yes	yes	yes	yes	26.
300	700	133000	yes	yes	yes	yes	22.5
250	900	124000	yes	yes	yes	yes	22.
300	700	66000	yes	yes	no	yes	16.2
200	900	66000	no	partial	no	yes	16.
250	1000	30000	no	yes	no	no	14.
250	900	89000	yes	partial	no	yes	9.
250	900	60000	yes	yes	yes	yes	8.5
150	600	25000	yes	partial	yes	yes	8.
300	900	41000	yes	yes	yes	yes	7.
300	700	50000	yes	no	no	yes	6.5
250	600	62000	yes	no	yes	yes	6.5
250	1070	66000	yes	partial	yes	yes	5.2
15	110	none	no	no	no	no	1.85
200	400	none	no	no	no	no	1.5
15	none	none	no	no	no	no	.7

[a] Characteristics given are as of January 1, 1964.

guages, they tend to restrict the use of problem-oriented languages in programming systems.

The auditor should not be lulled into a false sense of security by this temporary situation. The emerging concept of the business information system is on the threshold of significant breakthroughs. As the somewhat meager evidence tends to indicate, the auditor must begin to think in terms of more advanced control concepts in order to be able to cope with the problems of information systems as they proceed from segmented to more integrated systems based on mass-storage devices and sophisticated peripheral equipment incorporating the rapid advances being made in data transmission and collection.

Use of the full capacity of a central processing unit for a business information system requires attention to the concept of integrated data processing. The first step is to examine, in general outline, the peripheral equipment available as a link between the physical activity which gives rise to the input information and the central processing unit.

DATA COLLECTION AND TRANSMISSION

As early as 1949, Berkeley recognized the need for a balanced system. From the specifications of the various manufacturers, it is apparent that input-output speeds of on-line equipment were never designed for operating a high-speed business information system. If balanced systems in most business applications are to be achieved, increased emphasis must be given to the development of peripheral equipment which can convert data to machine-sensible form, thereby reducing the disparity between the computative and logical powers of the central processing unit and the capacity of the input channel.

The problem can logically be divided into two separate aspects. One aspect is concerned with data collection and conversion. The interaction of the business firm with the external environment and the internal activities of the firm itself give rise to vast amounts of data. Data must be collected in a logical and efficient manner and converted into a form suitable for processing. The second aspect of the problem involves transmission of the data from the originating point to the central processor. The auditor is vitally concerned with both aspects of this problem, for output is dependent on the quality of the input data as well as on the instructions given to the central processing unit.

The problem of data collection has been encountered by business firms since accounting records were first maintained. However, recent technological developments have focused attention on the importance of efficient measures for data collection. Since the cost of data collection can be a significant part of the total data-processing expenditure, and because reliable input data are essential, data collection is a major concern of the systems designer. Whatever the scheme, a business information system's data collection must meet three requirements: it must (1) accumulate significant data automatically; (2) convert raw data into machine-sensible form; and (3) maintain a record of the input data.

To survey the bewildering array of data collection equipment available today would be tedious and not very helpful to this study, but a review of some of the essential characteristics of data collection equipment is necessary to an understanding of the problems of the auditor dealing in computer processing. One of the earliest developments was the Flexowriter; this produces, as a by-product of typing invoices, a record on punched-paper tape. Adding machines also have been equipped with a device for transferring raw data to punched-paper tape. Monroe, Burroughs, and National Cash Register accounting machines have auxiliary units which produce punched-paper tape as a by-product. Addressograph-Multigraph Corporation uses punched-paper tape for input in producing embossed name-and-address plates as output. Cash registers can also be fitted with similar devices. Since paper tape can be used for input in most of the business-oriented computers which have been discussed, the possibilities of integration of the system are immediately apparent. In other cases, a conversion device is required to convert paper tape into punched cards, which are then used as input to the central processor, or into magnetic tape, which is then used as direct input to the computer. The concept of point-of-sale recording is a natural outgrowth of the technological developments of the Flexowriter concept.

In a basic application of data collection equipment for payroll, for example, recording stations are often located throughout the production departments of the plant. The timekeeping or dispatching stations serve as logical focal points for the collection and dissemination of pertinent information. Variable data are manually recorded on cards prepunched with such information as employee number, job number, operation, standard hours, and standard rates. In some instances, the manual insertion of variable data can be reduced considerably through the use of automatic time recording devices attached to the machines which perform the operations.

The data transmission process is the link between the data collection equipment and the equipment used to carry out the actual processing. From an auditing standpoint, data transmission does not pose as much of a problem as data collection does. From a design standpoint, however, data transmission is the key to efficient utilization of the central processor. A large computer is indivisible; if it is not kept busy—if an adequate and regular flow of data is not fed to it—the expense is spread over fewer useful hours and operational efficiency cannot be fully realized. Inadequate data transmission facilities inhibit the flow of data from branch plants and offices and tend to lead towards centralization of business organization. On the other hand, efficient data transmission facilities allow organizational flexibility and may actually encourage decentralization of decision-making functions, regardless of where the central processing unit may be located.

The chief concern of the auditor is with the reliability of data transmission and with the controls established for the operation of the system. Compatibility of components provided by different manufacturers may be a problem, but this is typically solved at the engineering level prior to implementation of the system. The reliability of data transmission is such that it does not pose a significant problem at the present state of equipment development; nor does the speed at which data transmission occurs, which may be equal to the speed of magnetic tape input (50,000 to 133,000 characters per second). The control problem of data transmission equipment is a matter of determining whether unauthorized interventions occur in the system between the data collection and the reception by the central processor during the input cycle.

Data collection and transmission can be viewed at two general conceptual levels. In the first instance, they can be seen as a one-way channel. In this situation, such as the payroll application previously discussed, the problem of feedback does not arise. The output follows other channels of data transmission. This setup constitutes a completely centralized system. Typically, this type of data communication occurs within local divisions of a business firm. In the more general case, the data collection station is also concerned with the results of the processing. For example, the data might be collected at the plant-wide level and transmitted to a central processor located in another city; the results of the plant activities are then transmitted back to the originator of the data. Depending on the design of the business information system, it is possible to operate in a decentralized organization with centralized data processing, and with appropriate data transmission the computer may actually facilitate the decentralization of decision making.

Mass-storage Devices

The second major building block in integrated EDP systems is the use of mass-storage devices. Magnetic core storage set up as an integral part of the central processing unit is more desirable, for the access time is measured in microseconds rather than the milliseconds of mass-storage devices. However, the cost of internal core storage is prohibitive for most systems, and other, less costly storage media must be used. Magnetic tape is an inexpensive way of storing machine-sensible data, but, unfortunately, the process of searching a magnetic tape file for specific information requires a prohibitive loss of time. The ideal scheme seems to lie somewhere between these two extremes if information measured in millions of characters is to be stored at a cost which is not excessive in relation to the benefit to be obtained from its relative accessibility.

The earliest concept in mass-storage devices was developed by International Business Machines: the IBM 305 RAMAC for random-access storage. According to the manufacturer,

The 305 RAMAC is an electronic accounting system with calculating abilities and a random access memory unit. Information in the form of punched cards is entered (input) into the system through a card reader which converts the punched card coding into a code of electrical impulses. The impulses are transmitted to, and stored on, a magnetic drum in the processing unit of the system.

Information to be retained in the system may be stored for indefinite periods in the form of magnetic spots on tracks of the memory disks. These disks have a capacity of 5,000,000 alphamerical characters, in the form of 50,000 one-hundred character locations.[18]

The average access time of the 305 RAMAC is 10 milliseconds, which is slightly more than four times longer than access time to the magnetic drum, but RAMAC's size is several hundred times larger. On the other hand, the 305 RAMAC's access time compares very favorably with the average access time of searching a magnetic tape for one specific record—approximately two and one-half minutes.

Subsequent advances have included the recent development by National Cash Register Company of the National 315.

The truly unique feature of the National 315 is a new concept in random access data storage. This is the unit NCR has dubbed CRAM for Card Random Access Memory. Up to 16 magnetic card units may be operative in a system. Each unit contains 256 cards of mylar plastic, 14 inches long by $3\frac{1}{4}$ inches wide. . . . The 256 cards are permanently enclosed in a cartridge. (The cartridges are interchangeable for each job.) . . . The capacity of each cartridge is 5,600,000 alpha or 8,300,000 numeric characters.[19]

The CRAM feature offers distinct advantages over magnetic tape and its flexibility allows random or sequential processing. It is somewhat slower than disk storage, but by optimal programming the time can be reduced to approximately 192 milliseconds. Other manufacturers have also added mass-storage devices or disk files to their equipment packages. For example, Burroughs Corporation offers an On-line Disk File System with each storage module capable of holding 9.6 million characters and having access to any record in 20 milliseconds.

It would serve no useful purpose here to present an exhaustive review of the mass-storage devices which are appearing on the market today; it is sufficient to observe that many such units of various merits are presently available. It is the task of the systems designer to choose the one most suitable for his system; and it is the responsibility of the auditor to understand the basic principles involved so that he will be able to perform his audit procedures satisfactorily.

The principal problem with mass-storage devices is that updating a record erases the previous entry contained in the record; thus, al-

---

[18] International Business Machines Corporation, *In-line Electronic Accounting, Internal Control and Audit Trail,* General Information Manual (New York: IBM Corporation, 1958), p. 2.

[19] *Data Processing Magazine,* July, 1961, p. 6.

though current balances are available instantaneously, the need to pre-serve the audit trail presents certain difficulties. A second problem exists as the counter-coin to one of the major advances of random-access equipment: precisely because it accepts data in random fashion, thus precluding the need for prior sorting or organization of input documents, the auditor is put at a great disadvantage in source document verification and in tracing relevant transactions. (This problem will be considered more extensively in chapters v and vi.)

FUTURE DEVELOPMENTS IN BUSINESS COMPUTERS

A number of patterns evident in the progress which has been made in the past decade have salient implications for future developments:

(1) The apparent stability of the central processor.—In the past few years, central processing units have not changed appreciably. As a matter of fact, it appears that the recent increase in purchases of central processors has occurred to a considerable extent because concern about obsolescence is no longer a significant restraint. With the development of the solid-state computer, a level was reached which will not change in the relatively near future. The needs of the scientific as well as of the business community now focus more on the mass-storage problem than on the logical capacity of the central processor.

This situation is fortunate for the systems designer, for he can work in a somewhat more predictable environment than formerly. It also encourages the development of problem-oriented programming lan-guages and the use of these languages by increasingly large numbers of people. With the logical structure of the computer remaining in status quo, the public accounting profession may be able to develop for computer-oriented business information systems audit programs appli-cable for a relatively long period of time. With better than marginal payout highly likely, auditors will doubtless increasingly give more thought and energy to these projects.

(2) The development of mass-storage devices.—Many of the recent developments in computer technology have occurred in the area of mass-storage devices. In October, 1962, IBM announced the IBM 1440, described as a new concept in disk-file memory and storage sys-tems. It uses 14-inch disks capable of storing 3 million digits or alpha-betic characters in each pack of six disks. The computer takes only about two-tenths of a second to extract information stored anywhere in a pack. The six-disk packs are readily changeable, like phonograph records; one pack can be substituted for another in a few seconds. The National Cash Register's previously discussed CRAM is also a rela-

tively new innovation in the field of mass-storage devices. And the IBM System/360, announced in the spring of 1964, provides additional possibilities for mass-storage applications.

The system designer is entitled to assume that the economic objections to magnetic core storage and the relative inaccessibility of data stored sequentially on magnetic tape will eventually become relatively less significant. It appears certain that the need for this type of hardware is rapidly being met by current technological developments. Thus, systems of the future can have available relatively low-cost, high-speed, random access time equipment providing storage of information which is now feasible only on magnetic tape or punched cards.

(3) The problem of input-output equipment.—As has been noted, there is increasing concern with input-output bottlenecks which in many installations have limited the efficient use of the central processor. For example, in the original design of the IBM 1401 data-processing system, the central processing unit was completely unbuffered. Not only was the input limited to the card-read speed, but other processing was inhibited during the read-in process. While substantial progress can be expected in input-output speeds of on-line peripheral equipment, it appears the real progress will stem from the developments in data collection and transmission.

Communication between central processors and between central processors and satellite systems promises revolutionary changes in the data-processing systems of the future. These changes will not necessarily be introduced by the manufacturers of computer hardware, but may come from a number of other industries. American Telephone and Telegraph, for example, recently announced that it has developed a device that can transmit drawings, maps, charts, and documents over telephone lines. The multiplexing concept promises additional means of using a central processor more efficiently. With these developments, it seems relatively certain that the central processing units in future business information systems will be able to operate increasingly effectively and efficiently.

(4) The conceptual framework of the data-processing system.— A natural sequel to the development of data communication techniques is the implementation of integrated data processing. The conceptual framework discussed in chapter ii can actually become operational. One of the big problems in the design of integrated data-processing systems has been the lack of a frame of reference within which the system could be structured. The other problem is the task of justifying an integrated data-processing system from an economic standpoint. Given the conceptual framework and the requisite hardware, the task of de-

tailed design and implementation becomes of paramount importance. There is little doubt that in many instances a business information system rejected as uneconomical would become economical when fully operational. But the tremendous cost of detailed design and implementation must be recoverable in a reasonable period of time. The simple payout criterion used in the average case might look something like this:

$$\frac{\text{Cost of detailed system design} + \text{Cost of installation}}{\text{Annual savings from operation of integrated system}} = \begin{array}{l}\text{Estimated number} \\ \text{of years to recover} \\ \text{expenditure}\end{array}$$

If we assume that the business manager must insist on a payout within two to five years, it is the burden of the systems designer to prove his case in those terms. Since the expense of long periods spent on systems design increases the payout period, this may in many cases lead the designer to adopt a "satisficing" approach in the sense that fully integrated systems may not justify the cost of design and installation given the constraints under which the designer is operating. While the integrated data-processing system is theoretically possible, the practical limitations imposed by economic constraints may greatly inhibit its adoption.

(5) The compatibility of electronic data-processing components.— The suppliers of electronic equipment need to concentrate their efforts on insuring the compatibility of various components without undue changeover costs. And since the detailed design of business information systems utilizing electronic equipment forces the systems designer to develop subprograms, these, too, should be furnished by the equipment supplier. With additional experience in the field, equipment suppliers will become more sophisticated in supplying "software packages" with the equipment, and this should tend to lessen the detailed drudgery and cost of systems design. The compatibility problem and the lack of packaged programs will be solved or at least mitigated during the immediate future.

(6) The use of small computers.—There is a need for small computers so that the business firm of moderate size may be able to justify their use. At the present time, small computers are considered to be those that rent for less than $8,000 per month. This is hardly within the means of many business firms. Exactly what form or shape small computers may take is not entirely clear at present, but it is evident there will be considerable efforts to expand the market for electronic computers in the direction of the smaller firm. This need not be a matter

of serious concern for the auditor, since auditing procedures and techniques applicable to larger systems will presumably be applicable to the smaller computers as well. It is mandatory that the public accounting practitioner keep himself informed on the latest developments of this area so that, in turn, he may guide his clients to take advantage of electronic aids that become available.

(7) The use of the "service bureau."—Electronic equipment manufacturers are becoming increasingly aware of the need to supply equipment for use on a part-time basis for customers whose needs do not justify full-time use of existing computers. Gordon A. Lowden, executive vice-president of National Cash Register Co., noted in November, 1962, that his firm would equip its 320 offices in the United States "with electronic data processing equipment to handle work for customers whose needs don't justify purchase or lease of larger computers."

The public accounting practitioner must keep his clientele informed of the possibilities of using "service bureau" equipment to process data. In most instances system design is minimized in this type of application, and therefore the conversion costs which exist in lease or purchase of computers does not become of primary importance. The trend towards service bureau operations will in many cases allow firms in the same industry to share the costs of program development to their mutual benefit. The potentials of this approach are almost without limit. One study has already developed such a plan for cost analysis in residential institutions for children.[20]

The evolving concepts of business information systems and trends in computer technology constitute the underlying forces contributing to the development of processing business data. Having reviewed them, we can now turn to a review of the development of auditing theory and practice and an appraisal of the current situation. We will then be ready to analyze the impact of the computer on auditing procedures and techniques.

---

[20] Martin Wolins, director, *A Manual for Cost Analysis in Residential Institutions for Children* (Berkeley, Calif.: California State Department of Social Welfare and Child Welfare League of America, 1962). See also Wayne S. Boutell, "The Implementation of Uniform Standards of Reporting for National Voluntary Agencies," *Accounting Review*, XXXVIII (July, 1962), 406-409.

IV

Auditing In A
Changing Environment

This chapter's brief review of important developments that have shaped auditing theory notes some of the early historical concepts, identifies the social forces which have influenced its development, and evaluates auditing standards, procedures, and techniques in the light of current practice.

It is not clear that any useful purpose is served by attempting to define "auditing"; indeed a definition without specifying a time dimension would lead to confusion. In itself, for example, the etymology of the word gives a false impression of its full current meaning. The word comes from the Latin *auditus*, a hearing, and in its earliest usage, during the time of the Normans in England, the relationship of the oral examination to auditing was quite clear. Today, the auditor's insistence on verifiable, objective evidence is quite different from the original idea of an oral examination. However, the historical concepts of auditing provide a useful background for present purposes.

THE CONCEPT IN ANTIQUITY

Since the time of the Babylonians and Assyrians, society has expressed concern for the safety of assets entrusted to public officials. Early concepts of auditing were concerned largely with the problems of communicating information pertinent to this trust to the ruling monarch or to the public generally. There was also concern for private trusts. One of the Laws of Hammurabi, *ca.* 2200 B.C., specified: "If a man desires to deposit with another, he shall exhibit before elders, draw up a contract, and then make deposit."

One of the main contributions of the Grecian civilization to the development of auditing theory was the concept of the so-called public audit. For example, during the building of a temple in Athens, interested persons could review the costs of construction by examining a marble tablet placed in front of the construction, showing the cumulative amount expended up to the beginning of the current year, the sums expended during the current year, and the total expended to date.

Further evidence of the emergence of a specific auditing function is found in the history of manorial England. The principal focus of the productive resources of England from the twelfth to the seventeenth centuries lay in the manorial estates. The reeve was the accountant of the manor. His work was subject to scrutiny by the lord of the manor or by his appointed administrator, the bailiff. The auditor of the manor was not an independent person, but he did perform a function somewhat analogous to that performed by auditors today. In some instances audit programs were set up, and criteria were established for the guidance of the auditor in determining, for example, the consumption of salt in relation to the number of pounds of meat processed, or the disposition of the hides of cattle that died or were killed prematurely.

The early concepts of auditing can be grouped roughly into two broad general classes. In the first instance, the audit consisted of a public interrogation of the performance of governmental officers by representatives of society. With the rise of private enterprise, the emphasis was similar to the attest function presently ascribed to certified public accountants. In this latter case, the bailiff examined and tested an account of stewardship for the benefit of his employer, the lord, who in the larger manors was not able to keep in close personal touch with daily financial affairs.

THE RISE OF THE PROFESSIONAL AUDITOR IN ENGLAND

As a result of the rise of commerce during the Middle Ages and of the embryonic stirrings of the Industrial Revolution, the English manor lost its self-sustaining status. The rise of the village and the growth of trade with the Continent foretold the downfall of the manorial system and the rise of the commercial and industrial firms of the eighteenth century. But England's experience in feudal days provided a suitable method for effectively supervising delegated responsibilities in the later period—the audit. A. C. Littleton[1] discusses the reasons for the intervention by the government in the nineteenth century, but the development of statutory audit requirements resulted essentially from public discontent with eighteenth-century stock speculations.

By the last quarter of the nineteenth century, the British government had given its full support to the concept of auditing, and the profession

---

[1] A. C. Littleton, *Accounting Evolution to 1900* (New York: American Institute Publishing Co., 1933), pp. 288-292.

was well established. In the model set of articles of association which were to apply to all companies registered under the British Act appeared the requirement that "The Accounts of the Company shall be examined and the Correctness of the Balance Sheet ascertained by One or more Auditor or Auditors to be selected by the Company in General Meeting."[2] However, the government apparently required only an examination of the balance sheet of the qualifying corporation. There were some provisions relating to independence, but little was said about the professional qualifications of the auditor. Nevertheless, for the first time, a definitive statement of the objectives of an audit of a business firm appears, and from this came the first tentative steps toward development of auditing standards. C. A. Moyer has expressed the rationale underlying British audits as follows:

It is generally recognized that auditing in Great Britain had been instituted to a great extent by specific statutory requirements. The principal function of an audit was considered to be an examination of the report of stewardship of corporation directors, and the most important duty of the auditor was to defect fraud. The search for defalcations resulted in a minute, painstaking check of the bookkeeping work done by the employees of the client. Almost all of the time of the auditor's staff was devoted to checking footings and postings in detail, in looking for bookkeeping errors, and in comparing the balances in the ledger with the trial balance and with the statements.[3]

EARLY DEVELOPMENTS IN THE UNITED STATES

Specific federal statutory auditing requirements did not exist in the United States until 1933. As a result, the development of the auditing profession in this country progressed slowly.

What little auditing was done in the United States before 1900 was influenced directly by British precedents. While the American Association of Public Accountants was formed in 1887, it was composed almost exclusively of accountants practicing in New York. A national voluntary organization did not emerge until 1916, when the American Association of Public Accountants authorized the incorporation of the American Institute of Accountants (subsequently the American Institute of Certified Public Accountants).[4] The Institute was created in

---

[2] H. C. Edey and Prot Panitpakdi, "British Company Accounting and the Law 1844-1900," reprinted in A. C. Littleton and B. A. Yamey, *Studies in the History of Accounting* (London: Sweet & Maxwell, Ltd., 1956), p. 363.

[3] C. A. Moyer, "Early Developments in American Auditing," *Accounting Review*, XVI (Jan., 1951), 3-8.

[4] Carl H. Nau, "The American Institute of Accountants," *The Journal of Accountancy*, XXXI (Feb., 1921), 105.

response to a felt need for an authority to control the practices of the profession without resort to statutory regulation. By 1921, Carl H. Nau was able to observe that "The American Institute of Accountants has already achieved such a standing among the better-informed business functionaries that membership therein is of greater value to the practitioner than the possession of the C.P.A. degree from most, if not all, of the states of the union."[5]

The first official act of the Institute was preparation of a memorandum on procedure, at the request of the Federal Trade Commission, which appeared in the April, 1917, issue of the Federal Reserve *Bulletin.* The purpose of the memorandum was to encourage standardization of the financial statements submitted to bankers for credit purposes; it also provided a program for verification of items and uniform compilation of statements.[6] Twelve years later, the memorandum was revised and republished under the title of "Verification of Financial Statements." Even in this revised version, however, there appears to be little if any change in the concept of auditing as originally viewed by the British statutory authority. For example, under the heading of General Instructions the following statement appears:

The scope of the work indicated in these instructions includes a verification of the assets and liabilities of a business enterprise at a given date, a verification of the profit-and-loss account for the period under review, and, incidentally, an examination of the accounting system for the purpose of ascertaining the effectiveness of the internal check.

This statement is almost indistinguishable from its counterpart in the model set of the articles of association given in the British Act. The examination of the system of internal check is included only as an afterthought, not as a condition precedent to the preparation of the audit program.

Although the American Institute of Accountants' official pronouncements did not blaze new trails in auditing theory and practice, some members of the profession were critical of existing practices. They attempted to stimulate creative thinking along more productive lines. Indeed, as early as 1912, prior to the formation of the Institute, Robert H. Montgomery, a partner in Lybrand, Ross Bros., and Montgomery, published his *Auditing Theory and Practice,* which strongly criticized accepted doctrines. He argued that three-fourths of the audit time typi-

---

[5] *Ibid.,* p. 106.
[6] American Institute of Accountants, *Verification of Financial Statements* (rev. ed.; Washington, D.C.; Federal Reserve Board, 1929), preface, p. v.

cally was spent on detailed checking of the extant records, but that
three-fourths of the defalcations actually occurred as a result of a
failure to record income transactions.[7] A decade later, Montgomery
suggested that the basis of deciding whether a detailed audit should
be made or whether a balance sheet audit would accomplish the desired
end depends to a considerable extent upon the existence of a satisfactory system of internal check.[8] In England, Lawrence R. Dicksee had
made a similar point in 1907.[9]

The first federal law to have a significant impact on the auditing
profession was the Securities Act of 1933. This act required registration
of securities to be offered to the public in interstate commerce, further
stipulating that the financial statements included in the registration
statement be certified by an independent or certified accountant. Lia-
bility provisions relating to the auditor compelled a self-evaluation of
the profession, and some agreement as to what constituted a proper
examination of financial statements under the requirements of the act.
In a letter to the New York Exchange dated December 21, 1933, the
Special Committee on Co-operation with Stock Exchanges of the
American Institute of Accountants emphasized that accountants, in
cases where they do not make a detailed audit, should regard it as a
part of their duty to inquire into the system of internal check.[10] The
committee cited the 1929 pamphlet, "Verification of Financial Statements." By conveniently deleting the word "incidentally," the committee nullified the original intention of the 1929 publication relegating
internal check to a minor role in the conduct of an audit examination.
The distortion of the 1929 document was apparently overlooked; at
least there is no record of any objection to this shift in emphasis, which
did, in any case, represent some progress in the thinking of the members of the profession.

The McKesson-Robbins case of 1938 had a profound influence on
the development of auditing standards. A summarization of the findings issued by the Securities and Exchange Commission states:

We are convinced by the record that the review of the system of internal
check and control at the Bridgeport offices of McKesson & Robbins was
carried out in an unsatisfactory manner. The testimony of the experts

---

[7] Robert H. Montgomery, *Auditing Theory and Practice* (New York: Ronald
Press, 1912), p. 258.

[8] Robert H. Montgomery, *Auditing Theory and Practice*, (3d ed.; New York:
Ronald Press, 1922), p. 62.

[9] Lawrence R. Dicksee, *Auditing* (London: Gee & Co., 1907), p. 39.

[10] American Institute of Accountants, *Audits of Corporate Accounts* (New York:
American Institute of Accountants, 1934), p. 40.

leads us to the further conclusion that this vital and basic problem of all audits for the purpose of certifying financial statements has been treated in entirely too casual a manner by many accountants. Since in examinations of financial statements of corporations whose securities are publicly owned the procedures of testing and sampling are employed in most cases, it appears to us that the necessity for a comprehensive knowledge of the client's system of internal check and control cannot be overemphasized.[11]

The American Institute of Accountants reacted promptly. In September, 1939, the Institute issued a report adopted by the membership, "Extensions of Auditing Procedures." It is interesting to note that this 1939 document did not discuss the problem of internal control, however. The suggestion made by the Securities & Exchange Commission relating to confirmation of accounts receivable and the physical observation of inventories was covered extensively. But the point quoted above was not covered in the Institute's pronouncement.

INTERNAL CONTROL

Ten years later, in 1949, the Committee on Auditing Procedures issued a special report entitled *Internal Control*. For the first time, and presumably with the sanction of the Institute membership, an official representation of the profession discussed this problem. Although the report was directed primarily toward specifying the responsibility of the public accountant for matters relating to internal control, the document is more broadly significant as an historic step in the development of auditing theory. Perhaps the one statement in *Internal Control* that makes the change in the thinking of the profession most obvious is the assertion that "subsequent examination cannot be regarded as a substitute for the exercise of proper controls in the actual handling of transactions."[12]

Subsequently, the Committee on Auditing Procedures in 1954 issued another special report, *Generally Accepted Auditing Standards, Their Significance and Scope*. One of the ten standards adopted in this report again referred to internal control: "There is to be a proper study and evaluation of the existing internal control as a basis for reliance

---

[11] "A Summary of the Findings of the Securities and Exchange Commission," reprinted in Howard A. Stettler, *Auditing Principles* (Englewood Cliffs, N.J.: Prentice-Hall, 1961), Appendix B., pp. 725-734.

[12] The American Institute of Accountants, *Internal Control* (New York: American Institute of Public Accountants, 1949), p. 6.

thereon and for the determination of the resultant extent of the tests to which auditing procedures are to be restricted."[13]

The most recent pronouncement on internal control was released in October, 1958, as Auditing Bulletin No. 29, *Scope of the Independent Auditor's Review of Internal Control.* By the time this document appeared, the literature on the subject of internal control had become rather voluminous, and many decisions of auditing procedure had come to hinge, more or less explicitly, on evaluation of the system of internal control. It was felt necessary, therefore, to issue a formal pronouncement summarizing the position of the professional organization, now renamed the American Institute of Certified Public Accountants. The major conclusion follows:

In the ordinary examination, the selection of auditing procedures, their timing, and the determination of the extent to which they should be followed will depend largely upon the auditor's judgment of the adequacy and effectiveness of the internal controls. This judgment is arrived at as the result of his study and evaluation (which may involve testing, observation, investigation and inquiry) of those internal controls which, in his opinion, influence the reliability of the financial records.[14]

In reflecting upon these developments in auditing theory and practice, it becomes apparent that the principal change was a matter of the emphasis placed upon the system of internal control and the consequences of this emphasis on audit procedures employed in the examination of accounts. The problem of internal check was not mentioned prior to 1900, but by 1958 internal control had become of paramount importance in the conduct of an examination.

The quality and effectiveness of internal control does not affect merely the amount and detail of an audit; it also changes the timing of the examination. In the early stages of development, auditors performed their review only after the year under examination was over. With emphasis on internal control, it is now opportune—indeed, necessary—to perform many of the audit procedures prior to the end of the year.

It is not clear, however, that all accountants are in agreement as to exactly what constitutes a system of internal control or what is meant by the efficiency of the system. The 1949 special report of the Committee on Auditing Procedure defines internal control as "the plan of or-

---

[13] The American Institute of Certified Public Accountants, *Generally Accepted Auditing Standards, Their Significance and Scope* (New York: American Institute of Certified Public Accountants, 1954), p. 13.

[14] The American Institute of Certified Public Accountants, *Scope of the Independent Auditor's Review of Internal Control,* Accountants Auditing Bulletin No. 29 (New York: The Institute, 1954), p. 37.

ganization and all of the coordinate methods and measures adopted within a business to safeguard its assets, check the accuracy and reliability of its accounting data, promote operational efficiency, and encourage adherence to prescribed managerial policies."[15] But it is not certain that the definition means the same thing to each practitioner. Generally, internal control is construed rather narrowly by the accounting profession. "Plan of organization" is taken to mean "plan of organization of the accounting department" as subsequently defined in Bulletin No. 29, which attempts to make a distinction between accounting controls and administrative controls. The more recent report goes on to stress that administrative controls need be examined only if in the judgment of the auditor they have a direct bearing upon the reporting practices of the company under examination. "Operational efficiency" and "prescribed managerial policies" are also susceptible of variable interpretation. To the practitioner, these phrases refer in the main to the accounting department only. According to Peloubet and Heaton, "the composite picture of auditing done by business employees is called the system of internal control."[16] But according to Mautz and Sharaff in *The Philosophy of Auditing,* the definition of internal control, properly construed, is so broad that the duty assigned to the independent auditor extends well beyond the area of capacity in which he has regarded himself as competent. Few, if any, practicing public accountants would claim the competence to review, for example, the effectiveness of training programs, time and motion studies, or quality controls which comprise a part of the system of standards whereby an effective system of internal control must be judged.[17]

In order to place the idea of a system of internal control in appropriate perspective from the standpoint of the public accounting practitioner, it may be viewed as a sub-classification of the accounting system, which in turn is a part of the information system of the business firm. Conceived in this way, internal control can be said to have three principal objectives: (1) to safeguard the assets of the firm; (2) to prevent intentional or unintentional mistakes; and (3) to insure adherence to management policies. The internal control concept will be more comprehensible and usable to the auditor in the field if he views the operation of the system in terms of its goals, Thus, we now turn, within such a framework, to the practical problems of the auditor in evaluating the effectiveness of the system of internal control.

[15] A.I.A., *Internal Control*, p. 6.
[16] Sidney W. Pelobuet and Herbert Heaton, *Integrated Auditing* (New York: Ronald Press, 1958), p. 6.
[17] R. K. Mautz and Ha A. Sharaf, *The Philosophy of Auditing* (Menasha, Wis.: American Accounting Association, 1961), p. 144.

THE AUDITOR'S FUNCTION

Given the three objectives of internal control listed above, the auditor has some guidelines for evaluating the system of internal control. Assuming for the moment that the auditor is able to make an evaluation of the system of internal control, how does he use this evaluation in the further conduct of his examination? In terms of current practice, it appears that the auditor must proceed as follows: (1) Determine the extent of the system of internal control by questioning, examination of accounting manuals, procedural flow charts, and organization manuals. (2) Test the system of internal control to insure that the system as outlined by management is in fact operating in the prescribed fashion or with insignificant deviations. (3) Design the audit program for the remainder of the examination based upon the system of internal control as it actually operates. (4) Carry out the remainder of the audit procedures and express an opinion on the fairness of the financial statements. These steps are sequential; they must be completed in the order given above, for each succeeding step depends on the previous one.

The series fulfills the field work auditing standards prescribing the three basic mandates of conducting an examination in the field: (1) adequate planning, (2) appropriate study and evaluation of the existing internal control, and (3) examination of competent evidential matter. These standards of field work are the guideposts used today for examination of financial statements.

A new question has arisen in the light of recent technological developments: What changes, if any, might—or should—now be made in these auditing standards? Although it is doubtful if the standards themselves will change within the foreseeable future, it is certainly probable that the degree of emphasis placed on each of the standards may well change. In the 1930's, although auditing standards were not explicitly stated, their order of priority was apparently (1) adequate planning, (2) examination of competent evidential matter, and (3) study and evaluation of the existing internal control. Since 1954 there has been a decided shift of emphasis; it now appears that study and evaluation of internal control has achieved top status as the basis of efficient and satisfactory examination.

Full appreciation of the significance of the shifting auditing emphasis requires clear recognition of the distinction between auditing standards and auditing procedures. The 1954 pronouncement of the American Institute of Certified Public Accountants on *Generally Accepted Auditing Standards* explains this distinction as follows:

Auditing standards may be said to be differentiated from auditing procedures in that the latter relate to acts to be performed, whereas the former deal with measures of the quality of the performance of those acts, and the objectives to be attained in the employment of the procedures undertaken.

To be sure, there is a close relationship between standards and procedures—and, as this discussion has already intimated, the influences are not in one direction only. Along with the current change in the emphasis on auditing standards, substantial changes in the underlying auditing procedures have already taken place, too, and it is almost certain that additional substantial changes will take place in the future.

The impact of electronic data-processing equipment on auditing procedures clearly involves the auditor's review of the system of internal control, as defined in the limited sense of accounting system controls. In order to evaluate the effectiveness of the system design ,the auditor must keep several general criteria in mind: (1) separation of the physical control of assets and the accountability for the assets; (2) adequate internal check points for testing the reliability of quantitative data; and (3) frequent use of external check points for comparing internal results with those obtained from sources outside the accounting department. If the auditor is satisfied that the system design meets these criteria, he is then obligated to test the operation of the system. It is at this point that observation of the accounting procedures becomes paramount. In the typical case, the auditor conducts his tests sometime during the year under review. The actual observation of the procedure, together with appropriate tests of the mathematical accuracy, gives the assurance that there is little chance for error in handling the source data which serves as the basis for the actual accounting entry.

It is important to note in this review of current practice that it embodies an on-going concept, as opposed to an *ex post facto* concept. This is the key emphasis of the theory of auditing as it is now conceived by the public accounting profession. This view makes it mandatory to conduct the review of the system of internal control on an interim basis in order to complete the examination of the year-end financial statements.

COMMENTS ON PUNCHED CARD ACCOUNTING

In connection with punched card accounting, there has been some discussion of the extent to which the earlier system of internal control is disturbed by the introduction of mechanical equipment. In a recent monograph, *The Audit and the Punched Card,* Corcoran and Istvan made the following observation:

Punched card equipment has made internal control more complex and even more important. This is true because the tabulating department incorporates in one section many of the accounting functions . . . formerly divided among the employees of the accounting department. The same person, for instance, may both write checks and maintain the general ledger, and might not, therefore, require the collusion of a fellow employee to abstract funds.[18]

Although Corcoran and Istvan proceed to point out that electric accounting machine (punched card) equipment can have a beneficial effect on internal control by eliminating transcription errors, they note that it is not an unmixed blessing. Errors made in reproducing source documents are reflected in all segments of the processing operation. Hence the auditor must emphasize input-output checks in his audit program.

Another comment made in the monograph is extremely important in regard to assessing the auditor's role in the evaluation of the system of internal control:

Internal control may suffer also where the tabulating supervisor is considered the most informed accounting person in the organization and is, therefore, granted unlimited authority—authority which enables him to interfere with established controls outside of the tabulating department.

The conclusions of Bulletin No. 29, wherein the Committee on Auditing Procedure stresses the subsidiary role of administrative controls in the evaluation of the system of internal control, would have to be somewhat modified if the Corcoran and Istvan view were to be accepted at face value. That is, whenever the auditor encounters a punched card installation, he must do more than merely examine the accounting controls of the organization: he must also examine the administrative controls. This requirement arises because the introduction of EAM equipment has placed unprecedented potential power in the hands of the tabulating supervisor. At least one criterion—adequate internal check points for testing the reliability of quantitative data—may be drastically changed by the introduction of this equipment. It is also possible that another of the criteria, the independence of accounting responsibilities,

---

[18] Wayne A. Corcoran and Donald F. Istvan, *The Audit and the Punched Card, An Introduction,* Bureau of Business Research, Research Monograph No. 101 (Columbus, Ohio: The Ohio State University, 1961), p. 22.

must be reassessed in the light of conversion to mechanical equipment.

Corcoran and Istvan suggest a partial solution to the problem they raise:

In reviewing the internal control when punched card equipment is in question it is especially important to ensure that control totals are established outside the accounting department. Furthermore, the checking of machine lists to the controls should be done by someone other than the tabulating machine operators. In the same vein, it is vital to establish controls that will ensure that all documents reach the tabulating department without duplication, and that if changes or corrections are made, they are made with proper authorization in a written form that reaches both the tabulating department and the controls external to the tabulating department.

EDP AND CURRENT TEXTBOOKS ON AUDITING

Comparison of recent editions of auditing textbooks' viewpoints regarding the impact of electronic data processing on audit standards and procedures reveals some interesting differences.

The 1957 edition of *Montgomery's "Auditing"* offers the following conclusions in the section on "Machine Bookkeeping":

Although the mechanics of auditing have to be adapted to machine bookkeeping, the fundamental purposes of auditing remain the same. Difficulties may arise in preserving a trail that can be audited, and the auditor will be forced to use his ingenuity in following information from the ultimate results back to original data. Internal accounting control will probably be affected, but it may not be weakened if proper division of duties is maintained; in fact, it may be strengthened since the mathematical accuracy of electronic machines is infinitely greater than that of human beings.

This view is typical of the early reaction of the auditing profession to electronic data processing. The tendency to rely on conventional "audit trail" techniques seems to have been predominant. An expectation of possible strengthening of the system of internal control was also typically expressed by practitioners and text writers. The date of the Montgomery text is significant; as earlier material in this study showed, even as recently as 1957 very little progress had been made in business applications of electronic computers.

A more recent textbook on auditing, the 1962 edition of Holmes' *Basic Auditing Principles,* asks: "In what ways are audit procedures changed when punched card or electronic equipment is used?" Holmes' answer reflects the growing impact of EDP technology:

The principles of auditing remain unchanged under any accounting system, but the application of recognized audit procedures is changed. With punched card and electronic applications in operation, the auditing follows the pattern of a thorough examination of internal control and of the programming, followed by tests to determine that the internal control and the programming are being followed and that the results are correct. . . . As the application of electronic analyses increases, auditing will become more and more an analysis of internal control and programming, followed by tests of the programming.

But this view somewhat confuses the issue by simultaneously considering punched card systems and electronic data-processing systems. Unfortunately, what Holmes means by a "thorough examination of the programming" is not made clear in any subsequent discussion, although this would seem to be a vital part of the change which is occurring in audit procedures.

Other recent writers also have mentioned—usually only briefly—electronic data processing and its effect upon internal control. Meigs' *Principles of Auditing* (1959) concentrates on examining controls which operate outside the data processing center. These, he says, are evaluated for the purpose of determining the adequacy of the system of internal control as it applies to the data-processing operation. He provides no detailed discussion of the changes, if any, in audit procedures or in audit standards. Settler's *Auditing Principles* (1961) devotes part of a chapter to the subject of electronic data processing. But he does not treat the matter as an integral part of the over-all audit procedures. Stettler refers to the completeness of the first eighteen chapters of his text, and then discusses EDP under "Other Audit Considerations" in chapter xix. In essence, Stettler stresses the need for reviewing data-processing controls and suggests that in some cases the computer program itself could be reviewed by comparing parallel operations of the computer and the manual system during the early installation phase of the system. However, he gives no detailed suggestions for the types of controls which are desirable. Peloubet and Heaton, in their *Integrated Auditing* (1958), suggest that the auditor should understand machine controls and proof totals as a necessary ingredient to the client's accounting system.

Auditing standards and procedures have not, then, remained static. Significant changes have occurred in the emphasis placed on the review of the system of internal control in the conduct of an examination. The focus has shifted from an *ex post facto* concept to one in which much of the examination is conducted during the year under review. Many underlying factors have caused this shift in emphasis, one of the principal contributors to the trend being the increasing complexity of business firms. The greater emphasis on the income statement as opposed to the balance sheet and the reaction of the auditor to this viewpoint have also been important.

Review of the system of internal control has assumed primary importance not only in shaping the course of the examination, but also in determining the auditing procedures used during subsequent steps in the examination. There is little doubt that the system of internal control as currently understood by the auditor is undergoing rather drastic changes. It is equally clear that, to date, the American Institute of Certified Public Accountants has reacted only negligibly to this change. Neither have the standard textbooks contributed substantially to the development of new concepts of the system of internal control, or even to preliminary critical review of current concepts. The subject is relegated to a minor role in virtually all current editions of auditing texts.

The public accounting profession has advanced rapidly in response to the needs of the business community. But its movement has been almost entirely reaction to developments, not leadership. Given the technological improvements of the past few years, the profession clearly has an opportunity to assume a position of leadership in the business community in the development of business information systems.

As viewed by the practitioner, the system of internal control is only a narrow concept concerned primarily with accounting controls, and secondarily with administrative controls in certain circumstances. There is a serious question as to whether the auditor should expand his efforts in this connection, and thereby perform a much greater service both for the client and for the profession. With a broader concept of the business information system, the practitioner would be in a better position to conduct a "management audit," which would expand his services to the client and enhance the prestige and contribution of the public accounting profession.

V

Auditing Theory And Practice

The thinking of that portion of the public accounting profession which has had experience with clients using a computer to process accounting data will probably increasingly influence the entire profession and its role in the business community. Initially, the auditor tended to view the computer as an obstacle to be overcome or circumvented before he could express an opinion on the financial statements. More recently, there seems to be a feeling that the computer may actually strengthen internal controls and may be of assistance in conducting the examination. This latter point of view is considerably more progressive. But, as we have seen, even the current literature unfortunately muddles the traditional approach and the more progressive viewpoint. It also largely overlooks another very important element, the matter of timing. As was briefly noted earlier, the stages of progress in the evolutionary development of EDP business information systems have not been satisfactorily reconciled with the suggested solutions for the auditing problems. It is small wonder, then, that the reader becomes confused. It is the task of this chapter to sort out the significant statements in the literature and to attempt to create a more cohesive picture of the problem.

Part of the confusion which exists in the relatively new field of electronic data processing and auditing is the uncertainty whether the literature tends to reflect the viewpoint of the majority of the public accounting practitioners. In view of this uncertainty, a survey was made of the procedures which are actually used in auditing business-oriented computer installations today. This was accomplished by means of a questionnaire which was circulated among the public accounting firms concerned with this problem. Comparison of the significant points in the literature with the summary of existing practices presents some interesting contrasts. The lack of uniformity in the thinking of the public accounting profession is obvious.

[60]

Electronic Data Processing and Auditing

Since 1956, a number of books have appeared dealing with the general use of computers for processing data for business firms. The earliest significant work, *Electronic Data Processing for Business and Industry,* by Richard G. Canning, appeared in 1956.[1] Canning's review of the pioneer installations of electronic systems pointed out the major lessons the respective managements had learned. In view of the limited number of business-oriented computers then in existence and the state of computer technology, it is not surprising that the problems which are of major concern today were not even considered by Canning. His major contribution was to provide a systematic framework for the design of a computer-oriented business system, a framework still relevant today.

The next significant work, which appeared in 1957, was written by Ned Chapin, systems analyst of the Stanford Research Institute.[2] The title of the book, *An Introduction to Automatic Computers,* does not adequately describe the subject matter which it covers. Although the greater part of the book is devoted to technical aspects of computer operation, the first definitive statement of the auditing problem is made explicitly. In essence, Chapin's major points about auditing can be stated as follows:

(1) The auditor must satisfy himself on the question of whether or not the source documents and vouchers constitute an accurate, fair, and complete record of the original transactions.

(2) He must satisfy himself that the computer input is an accurate, fair, and complete reflection of the original transactions as evidenced by the source documents.

(3) The auditor has to establish that the output of the automatic computer can be obtained, by the use of the program, from the input.

(4) The auditor must determine whether or not the program establishes a logical and acceptable relationship between the input and output of the computer.

(5) He will probably want to check on the separation of interest in the operation of the automatic computer.

(6) He will probably want to verify any changes that may have been made in the program.

(7) The auditor will probably want to verify that no irregular data are fed into the computer during the course of its data processing.

[1] Richard G. Canning, *Electronic Data Processing for Business and Industry* (New York: John Wiley & Sons, 1956).

[2] Ned Chapin, *An Introduction to Automatic Computers* (Princeton, N.J.: D. Van Nostrand Company, 1957).

(8) He will probably want to verify that adequate maintenance is done on the hardware of the computers.

(9) The auditor is really concerned only about the computer processing of information that substitutes for the traditional forms of processing.

Subsequent writers have tended to compartmentalize auditing problems into three major areas: (1) controls over input, (2) controls over processing, and (3) controls over output. All of these points were covered by Chapin in 1957. In addition, Chapin raised the problem of the unauthorized intervention of the console operator, the reliability of hardware, and the goals of auditing. These matters are still the subject for current debate.[3]

Neither the auditing textbooks discussed in chapter iv nor the books on accounting and electronic data processing provide any serious discussion of the auditing problems associated with electronic computers, with the one notable exception of Chapin's 1957 book. A pioneering effort of Felix Kaufman to bridge the gap between the auditor and the computer technician was published in 1961, *Electronic Data Processing and Auditing*.[4] But Kaufman's book is devoted to a consideration of the controls on electronic data-processing systems rather than to the auditing problems which are posed by the system. In the first chapter, Kaufman says:

A detailed consideration of the design of audit programs for electronic data processing systems is not attempted here. Such a development would be premature. Up to this time, the majority of electronic data processing installations have not affected auditing much because of the narrowness of applications, slowness in achieving integrated processes, and the time taken to establish new patterns and to shift old patterns to fit new methods. Under the circumstances, attempts to generalize about new programs would be to do in the abstract what has traditionally been accomplished by empirical methods.

Perhaps Kaufman's bias was justifiable at the time he wrote, for it is necessary to establish a frame of reference—a context of practice as well as of theory—before detailed consideration of the design of audit programs is attempted. The frame of reference Kaufman established is very useful to the public accounting practitioner and does provide a springboard for the formulation of appropriate audit procedures and

---

[3] See "Program of WJCC," afternoon session of May 1, 1962, held at Mark Hopkins Hotel, San Francisco.

[4] Felix Kaufman, *Electronic Data Processing and Auditing* (New York: Ronald Press, 1961).

techniques for reviewing electronic data-processing installations. But the fact remains that, up to the present time, no study has been made of the auditing problems. Several suggestions made in recent articles are relevant to this problem, however.

Articles on EDP and Auditing

In 1956 Price Waterhouse & Co. prepared *The Auditor Encounters Electronic Data Processing* at the request of International Business Machines.[5] This is a forward-looking statement which still has a great deal of relevance. Briefly, the Price Waterhouse report stressed the need for maintenance of "audit trails" as the primary means of auditing electronic data-processing systems. However, it also gave considerable attention to the establishment of controls within the equipment itself and in the writing of programs which would perform various editing functions, thereby increasing the reliability of the output. A rather novel approach was also suggested: establishment of an independent bureau, outside of the control of the data-processing group, to conduct a pre-audit of the input data and a reconciliation of the output of the data-processing system. This appears to be an extension of the functions of the internal auditor and has considerable merit for the strengthening of internal controls. Finally, this early work suggests the possibility of using the equipment in the audit itself, a development which has established the frame of reference for subsequent thinking.

Another early article of considerable interest is Clarence R. Jauchem's "Impact of Electronic Data Processing on Auditing,"[6] in which, for the first time, the battle lines were drawn regarding what approach should be adopted in auditing electronic data-processing systems. Jauchem makes explicit the conflict between

. . . two points of view regarding the immediate impact of electronic data processing on auditing. On one hand, there are some who feel there will be no change insofar as the auditor is concerned and the auditor can audit around the machine. On the other hand, there are some who feel that electronic data processing will have an immediate drastic effect on auditing and that elaborate training, including technical training in programming, should be undertaken at an early date for large segments of the auditing staff.

---

[5] International Business Machines Corporation, *The Auditor Encounters Electronic Data Processing,* General Information Manual (New York: IBM Corporation, 1956).

[6] C. R. Jauchem, "Impact of Electronic Data Processing on Auditing," *N.A.A. Bulletin,* XXXIX (May, 1958), 53-59.

A number of writers have stressed the importance of adequate internal control over data-processing operations. The initial impetus for
this concept seems to have come from the introduction of random-
access (mass-storage) equipment. In 1958, Price Waterhouse, again at
the request of International Business Machines, considered this development from the standpoint of internal control and the maintenance of
an adequate audit trail.[7] The basic problem with random-access equipment is that updating a total erases the previous total. Therefore, a
ledger does not contain all transactions that entered into the total, but
only the final balance in each account. This effectively eliminates the
detailed ledger record traditionally relied on by auditors. Moreover,
proof totals, which are useful in the batching concept, tend to disappear
within in-line electronic accounting systems. Kaufman is not particularly disturbed by these developments; he feels

. . . there is no need to be dismayed by the inability to apply control
totals, because the errors controlled by proof totals are minimized by
on-line transmission. These are the errors which occur during batching
and transmission. An error in recording an event is irrelevant to this
consideration because proof totals do not control those cases.

Kaufman's final observation obtains if consideration is given only to
that aspect of proof totals to which he refers. But proof totals are also
used for external confirmation of internal processing; hence, the elimination of proof totals creates substantial problems for the auditor. This
is the reason for the importance of emphasizing internal control aspects
of electronic data-processing systems.

There have been several attempts to classify controls which are important to auditors in the examination of an EDP system. Kaufman's
classification was perhaps the earliest:
  (1) Measures based upon the consistency of information.
  (2) Measures based upon the "meaning" of information.
  (3) Measures based upon comparisons of source data.
  (4) Measures based upon "outside" checks.
  (5) Organization of clerical work:
        (a) separation of duties;
        (b) coördination of paper work with physical processes.
Frank J. Curka also sets up five essential elements of internal control as
they relate to electronic data-processing systems:[8]

---

[7] International Business Machines Corporation, *In-line Electronic Accounting,
Internal Control and Audit Trail* (New York: IBM Corporation, 1958).
[8] Frank J. Curka, "The Effect of Electronic Data Processing on Auditing,"
N.A.A. Bulletin, XLIII (April, 1961), 85.

1. Division of duties and responsibilities among employees or groups of employees . . . [so] that no person has complete accounting control over substantially all phases of a business transaction.
2. Procedures [ensuring]consistent and accurate processing of the source data.
3. Procedures [ensuring] consistent and accurate processing of the data.
4. Intermediate review of documents and records by authorized employees.
5. Review and interpretation of the end results of the accounting system.

It is not clear exactly how the auditor is to apply the criteria Curka suggests. There is, in fact, a fundamental error in the concept of how data are processed by a computer in his first point, but essentially the criteria are sound as related to source data controls, processing controls, and output controls.

Robert F. Garland, writing in the *N.A.A. Bulletin* of July, 1962, suggests that internal controls normally take the form of (1) rules which act to prevent departure from management policy; (2) methods which feed back information regarding any departure, so that corrective action can be taken by management; and (3) actions which merely report performance as compared to budgets, established goals, previous periods, and the like. Garland's article then attempts to evaluate the ways in which computers strengthen internal control. He lists as salient features (1) the speed with which the computer can operate; (2) the complete system-wide uniformity of treatment of like items in computer systems, which contributes to internal control; (3) the logical power of the computer, making exception reporting feasible; (4) the ability of the computer system to accept system-wide changes; and (5) the ability of the computer to receive programming in anticipation of events which may occur in the future, thus allowing the executive of the internal control system to pre-plan for any circumstances the system may encounter. Garland's interpretation is certainly not within the context of the conventional definition of internal control. But regardless of how they are identified, the second, third, and fourth points are convincing. Points one and five cannot be construed as variables in internal control; speed is not a control factor unless coupled with feedback characteristics, and the ability to pre-plan is entirely dependent upon the systems designer and not upon the computer itself. But, on the whole, Garland does give some support to the argument that the use of computers by business firms may actually strengthen the controls of the business information system.

The only recent article devoted exclusively to the subject of electronic data processing and its impact on auditing procedures was

Arthur B. Toan, Jr.'s in June, 1960.[9] The implications of the auditor's choice of auditing procedures for auditing EDP systems are well-stated:

> . . . the auditor has a significant choice. He can, on the one hand, take advantage of his rights to put a brake on the rate of progress which can be made. He can, I believe, actually do this. On the other hand, he has an opportunity to contribute to this progress by imaginatively adjusting his approaches and his methods to the extent that he safely can. For the long-run reputation of the professional accountant, I would suggest that the latter course of action would be the safer one to follow.

Toan also suggests that the auditor use a model of internal control and develop audit procedures geared to testing this model. The logical structure of the model, he says, would indicate that the computer be used to conduct this test within specific limits. However, Toan does not follow through on this idea; he leaves unattended many serious questions about implementation. What is meant by the logical structure of the model is not clear; there appears to be no definite idea of what constitutes an adequate system of internal control. And, indeed, Toan admits that a great deal more consideration must be given to these problems; he concludes the article on this note:

> It is difficult to see how someone without a good working knowledge of both auditing and EDP can make a real contribution in these areas. I have a feeling that in most, if not all, firms knowledge of EDP is pretty well concentrated in management services departments. While a high degree of cooperation between the auditor and the management services representative will undoubtedly be beneficial, it is hard to see how the auditor's contribution can be as effective as when he himself understands the essential points of an EDP operation. While the auditor obviously need not be an EDP expert on the management services department level, I humbly suggest that those auditors whose clients are actively engaged in EDP should add a reasonable working knowledge of EDP to their own "tools of the trade."

Some additional evidence of the views of public accounting practitioners can be obtained from a series of talks given in May, 1962, at the special orientation program on information processing of The American Federation of Information Processing Societies in San Francisco. Three

---

[9] Arthur B. Toan, Jr., "The Auditor and EDP," *Journal of Accountancy*, CIX (June, 1960), 42-46.

speakers representing three national public accounting firms presented different points of view which can be briefly summarized as follows: [10]

(1) The primary purpose of auditing electronic data-processing systems is to test the company's computer program. This can be accomplished by simulating actual transactions with predetermined answers.

(2) The primary goal of the auditor is to use the computer to test the output of the client's program. For this purpose, an independent computer program, to be maintained under the control of the auditor, must be developed.

(3) The emphasis in auditing computer-oriented systems is to review the controls which the client maintains over his input, processing, and output.

The differences of emphasis are particularly clear in the respective procedures and techniques the speakers suggested for accomplishing audit objectives. One speaker emphasized the validity of the program, one emphasized the reliability of the output, and one emphasized the importance of controls over both program and output.

The federal government has also expressed a point of view regarding the auditing of EDP installations. The comptroller of the Air Force issued a *Guide for Auditing Automatic Data Processing Systems* on November 1, 1961. This publication distinguishes between the use of audit trail techniques and auditing "through the machine." But the Air Force document did not adopt any uniform approach to the auditing problem, so the *Guide* hardly contributes to clarification. The reader is left with the uneasy feeling that the procedures and techniques to be employed by the auditor are left, in the last analysis, to his own judgment. Moreover, the manual does not go beyond the major point made by the first speaker at the AFIPS meeting—the testing of the client's computer program by the utilization of simulated transactions.

The Internal Revenue Service has expressed grave doubts as to whether its agents will be able to audit automated systems effectively. This concern was discussed by Dean J. Barron, director of the IRS Audit Division in a talk before the IRS Automatic Data Processing Conference on October 23, 1961:

. . . the following should be a part of the system to provide an adequate audit trail:

---

[10] These speeches are not available in print. The quoted material is taken from notes made by the author.

(a) Master files, regardless of the media by which they are maintained, should be written out in detail at regular intervals, weekly, monthly, quarterly, semi-annually, or annually, depending upon the extent of the activity affecting them.

(b) All the information used to update the master files, including all additions, deletions, adjustments and changes, should be summarized and written out at the same periodic intervals as the master files.

(c) Adequate record retention facilities should be available for storing these print-outs as well as all applicable supporting documents for the period of time established by directives and contracts. Such facilities should allow reasonably easy access to these listings and records as required for audit purposes.

(d) The detail making up the control account balances, as in the area of accounts receivable, accounts payable, inventories, expenses, and income, should be written out at regular intervals.

(e) Clear and concise logical procedural directives should be available for audit examination, including up-to-date operator's logs and flow charts and block diagrams of all equipment operations.

These major points have been restated in the IRS's *Suggested Guidelines for Record Requirements for Taxpayers Relying on Automatic Data Processing Systems.* Apparently the Internal Revenue Service will expect taxpayers to maintain all conventional records which were maintained prior to the installation of electronic equipment. To do so cannot avoid creating difficulties with output and retention requirements. The approach of the Internal Revenue Service will probably be modified when experience has been gained in auditing installations of electronic computers.

Canada's chartered accountants, too, have been observing the impact of the electronic computer on business information systems. An article by W. L. MacDonald in the *Canadian Chartered Accountant* in September, 1962, appears to agree with the emphasis on controls:

. . . the auditor's attention should be directed away from vouching, for example, a substantial number of sales invoices of a given accounting period; or from verifying the arithmetical accuracy of accounting reports. Rather his attention should be directed towards a thorough review of the discipline over the computer department regarding programme changes and the daily operation of the equipment. The auditor should carry out a comprehensive review of the external controls over the computer department. The control features over input information will also merit a careful investigation. The interim audit of a computer installation will require a much larger percentage of the time to be assigned to the system review than to the vouching of individual transactions.

MacDonald seems to think that this change will require spending more time on the systems review. It is not clear whether this implies an over-all increase in the total audit hours of an engagement, but he certainly considers the computer to be an obstacle which the auditor must overcome in order to complete his examination properly. Although the end of MacDonald's article stresses the need for general knowledge of computer methods, this statement is difficult to evaluate in the light of his control emphasis in the body of the article.

A Critical Appraisal of the Literature

When the major points made by the various authors are assembled, it becomes clear that the traditional viewpoint of auditors generally prevails in the literature on auditing and electronic data processing: the auditor's principal function is to review transactions after they have happened; therefore, it is necessary to provide some readable media for referring to past transactions. A logical extension of this view is also common: emphasis on the importance of the audit trail in the consideration of systems design. Almost without exception, the writers consider the problem of the audit trail to be of primary importance. The extreme example is the Internal Revenue Service view referred to earlier.

The Price Waterhouse report cited earlier, *The Auditor Encounters Electronic Data Processing,* discussed the importance of external controls. It emphasized the realiability of the computer hardware; and errors due to malfunctioning of components have been rare (although a recent article does consider these so-called "quiet errors"[11]). Basically, current concern stresses the need to review the controls over the system as opposed to an analytical review of the data-processing system components. This notion of reviewing controls requires a lesser degree of sophistication with electronic equipment, and the average public accounting practitioner appears to be more receptive to this newer point of view. Nor is this emphasis on controls inconsistent with the maintenance of adequate audit trail. The combination of these two emphases probably represents the most acceptable theoretical point of view from the standpoint of current installation of electronic computers.

There is also some evidence in more recent articles that some constructive thinking is being devoted to the possibilities of auditing "through the computer." This is perhaps best stated by Toan in his 1960

---

[11] Felix Kaufman, "EDP Control Problems," *The Controller,* July, 1962, pp. 364-367.

article. Another article, which appeared in 1961, presents a case study of a computer audit program as it was actually utilized in connection with a payroll application.[12] This auditing-through-the-computer approach is not necessarily inconsistent with either the maintenance of conventional audit trail or the utilization of external controls, but in many instances may substantially reduce the necessity for audit trail.

These appear to be the main points which have been made in the literature on auditing and electronic data processing as EDP in business approaches the end of its first decade. The core deficiency as a professional literature is the lack of a common frame of reference within which the individual discussions can become meaningful. The reader is usually at a loss to orient his thinking to a particular model (often only vaguely implicit) of a business information system. For an auditor to think constructively about an auditing problem, he must first understand the system clearly. Insofar as an article is, in a sense, a substitute for experience, a specific environment—which is always considered in reviewing a practical situation—must be made known in discussions in the literature. The literature is generally inadequate in several other ways, too: in its typical failure to consider the timing factor, in its lack of distinction between in-line and batch-controlled systems, and in its confusion between normative and descriptive approaches.

There appears also to be considerable confusion between the systems approach and the auditing approach. Many writers deal almost exclusively with the problem of systems design, although purporting to to deal with auditing problems. The auditor is understandably concerned about his lack of knowledge of systems design and the apparent need for increased technical skills in order to cope with the problems of auditing computer-oriented business information systems. This concern distorts the true picture, and the natural reaction to the overcomplicated distortion appears to be to take recourse in the traditional and the familiar. This attitude on the part of the profession can inhibit the development of data-processing systems and may suppress the interest that the profession ought to be stimulating.

SURVEY OF PUBLIC ACCOUNTING PRACTICES

Although several of the authors already cited were public accounting practitioners, the possibility that the literature might not reflect ac-

---

[12] J. W. Oberfell, "Case Study of a Computer Audit Program in Action," *The Price Waterhouse Review*, VI (Summer, 1961), 40-48.

curately the current practices of the profession suggested investigation. Accordingly, as was mentioned earlier, a questionnaire was submitted to the relevant segment of the public accounting profession in order to determine the auditing procedures and techniques which they are following today. A copy of this questionnaire together with a summary of the findings is included as Appendix A.

The response to the questionnaire was very encouraging, particularly since an earlier survey undertaken by the Management Services Committee of the American Institute of Certified Public Accountants failed, in the Institute's view, to reveal the types of information sought. Out of the nine major public accounting firms included in the study reported now, seven firms responded.

The questionnaire was designed to be completed on a local office basis rather than for the accounting firm as a whole. Accordingly, the usual procedure was for the public accounting firm to select for the test those offices which had had experience with the installation and auditing of business-oriented computer systems. The various accounting firms returned from one to eight completed questionnaires.

The questionnaire was divided into two major parts, one dealing with the auditing environment and the procedures used to audit the records of clients using the electronic computers, the other concerned with the design and implementation of business-oriented computer systems. The transmittal letter suggested that the first part be completed by a partner on the audit staff and, if feasible, that the second part be completed by the manager of the management services department of the office.

The questionnaire was directed towards clients of the public accounting firms with annual sales volume in excess of $20,000,000. The number of client firms represented in the survey, classified by industry, is tabulated below:

Type of commodity or service	*Number of client firms*	*Percentage*
Manufacturing	549	43.2
Wholesaling	91	7.1
Retailing	79	6.2
Transportation	89	7.0
Communication, public utilities	66	5.2
Services	63	4.9
Government or governmental enterprises	17	1.3
Finance, insurance, real estate	234	18.4
Unclassified	85	6.7
Totals	1273	100.0

Data were obtained regarding the type of electro-mechanical or electronic equipment used by the business firms included in the survey. The following results were obtained:

Type of equipment	Number	Percent-age
Punched-card equipment	662	52.0
Tape-oriented computer	284	22.3
Use of service bureau	158	12.4
No electro-mechanical equipment	169	13.3
Totals	1273	100.0

The types of systems employed by the 284 firms using tape-oriented computers for processing data were distributed as follows:

Type of system	Number	Percent-age
Batch-controlled	172	60.6
Random-access (in-line)	35	12.3
Combination batch-controlled and in-line	44	15.5
Integrated data-processing	20	7.0
Unclassified	13	4.6
Totals	284	100.0

The reported total of integrated data-processing systems is not reliable since an adequate definition of IDP was not given in the questionnaire.

Some accounting functions appear to be relatively more adaptable than others to tape-oriented computers. A summary of the utilization of the computer by function follows:

Function	Number	Percent-age (N=284)
Payroll	234	82.4
Billing and accounts receivable	222	78.2
Accounts payable	100	35.2
Inventory control	135	47.5
Production control	56	19.7
Scientific research	41	14.4
All other functions	11	4.0

Preliminary investigation suggested grouping audit procedures and techniques into four general categories. Accordingly, two questionnaire questions (17 and 18) sought to determine to what extent these principal types of procedures and techniques were actually used in practice. Question 17 was directed expressly to firms using a batch-controlled system. A summary of findings follows:

Audit procedures and techniques	Always	Usually	Seldom	Never
Use of conventional audit trail records	14	5	5	0
Use of controlled data (test deck) to review client's computer program	1	10	6	5
Maintenance of a controlled copy of client's program tape to test periodically client's tape (or output)	0	1	8	14
Use of independent audit program, in problem-oriented language, prepared by public accounting firm for testing output of client's computer program	0	2	10	8
Review and testing of internal control and operating procedures	3	0	0	0

Current practice appears to be following a relatively elementary approach by stressing the maintenance of the audit trail as a necessity for auditing batch-controlled systems. The answers indicate that testing the client's program by use of a so-called "test deck" also enjoys considerable acceptance among the public accounting firms. Neither of these approaches requires any great deal of sophistication in computer technology or programming. Both indicate the tendency of the profession to perpetuate audit procedures employed prior to the advent of the business-oriented computer. This may be a matter of expediency or a matter of "inertia." The answers to a question (11) relating to the degree of proficiency of the audit staff are relevant:

Level of understanding	Number	Percent-age
Basic understanding of the internal logic of the computer, including ability to write in basic programming languages	192	8.4
General understanding of input-output equipment and some knowledge of internal controls built into the computer	565	24.6
General understanding of how computers function and ability to read and interpret "flow charts" and "block diagrams" of computer systems	640	27.9
Have none of the above	900	39.1
Totals	2297	100.0

Question 12 has the same alternatives of levels of understanding, but asks what degree of proficiency the respondent feels is desirable for staff accountants who audit EDP installations. Seventy-seven per cent of the replies indicate the desirability of at least a general understanding of the input-output equipment and some knowledge of the internal controls built into the computer. Question 11 responses, on the other hand, show that only 33 per cent of present audit staff meet this minimum desirable standard. Consequently, given the present level of sophistication of audit staff accountants, the only feasible solution for public accounting firms is to rely on auditing procedures which utilize a minimum amount of knowledge regarding business-oriented computers.

The inertia argument is reinforced by the fact that only 22.3 per cent of the firms with annual sales over \$20,000,000 have tape-oriented computers; hence, audit procedures for the remaining 77.7 per cent of these clients do not have to be revised to any great extent. Question 6 answers indicate that 79 per cent of the respondents agree that only minor changes in audit procedures are necessary when the client has either a punched-card system or a card-oriented computer.

Finally, a batch-controlled system lends itself very nicely to the maintenance of the conventional audit trail; this circumstance reinforces the public accountant's belief that audit procedures do not have to be altered appreciably. Although according to answers to another question (16) 61 per cent of the respondents indicate that it is necessary to review completely and revise audit procedures for clients who install a tape-oriented computer, the revisions do not extend to consideration of techniques which would allow the elimination of audit trail requirements.

Question 18 ("How often are the following techniques used in auditing . . .") poses alternatives identical to those of 17, but is directed to clients who have an in-line computer system. The contrast with the answers regarding the batch-controlled system is significant. A summary of the responses follows:

Audit procedures and techniques	*Always*	*Usually*	*Seldom*	*Never*
Use of conventional audit trail records	8	8	0	0
Use of controlled data (test deck) to review client's computer program	5	2	6	3
Maintenance of a controlled copy of client's program tape to test periodically client's tape (or output)	1	0	8	7
Use of independent audit program, in problem-oriented language, prepared by public accounting firm for testing output of client's computer	0	2	7	8
Review and testing of control procedures	1	0	0	1
No experience in auditing in-line EDP installations—9				

It is significant that of the 284 tape-oriented computer systems included in the survey only 99 (35 per cent) can be classified as in-line systems. Therefore the experience in auditing this latter type of system is much more limited than experience with the more common batch-controlled system, which accounts for 60 per cent of all the tape-oriented computer installations. Moreover, nine of the respondents indicated that they have not had experience in auditing in-line systems. In view of these factors, the results of question 18 must be considered as less than conclusive. But the general trend of the answers seems to indicate basic disagreement as to the best way of auditing an in-line system. Only 8 of the respondents indicate that they always insist on conventional audit trail requirements, but the others fail to indicate any adequate substitute. The consensus of practitioners therefore is very much in doubt on this issue. The answers to both questions 17 and 18 indicate that there is little or no use of programs designed to audit the client's computer programs. Apparently the problems inherent in either in-line systems or the more complex integrated data-processing systems have not become sufficiently widespread to warrant serious attention on the part of the profession.

There are indications throughout the answers to the questionnaires of an awareness of the importance of the review and testing of control procedures applicable to the data-processing system. How this is to be accomplished is not entirely clear, but from the responses to one question (19) it is apparent that the answer is not to be gleaned from the use of internal auditors. Only four respondents indicate that the reports of internal auditors are extremely useful in reviewing the internal controls of an EDP installation. As with the audit staff accountants, there is a serious question as to the competency of the internal auditors in the area of data-processing controls.

The question (21) concerned with expected developments in auditing tape-oriented computer systems revealed the following:

Development needed	*No. of replies*
Greater emphasis on internal and external data control	6
Use of test decks to review computer audit programs	5
Greater emphasis on procedure reviews and program testing	4
Surprise visits to observe computer operations	3
More effective utilization of internal auditors	2
Development of computer audit program in cooperation with the client	2
Increased knowledge on part of auditors	1
Use of computer programs written by the auditor	1

These suggestions substantiate the earlier observation that there will be increased emphasis on input controls, procedure reviews, and program testing. But only one respondent felt this development may occur through the use of computer programs written by the auditor.

By and large, then, the first part of the questionnaire shows that audit staff personnel of the public accounting practitioners have not yet had to face the problems of comprehensive data-processing systems to any great extent. It is equally clear that they have little time for constructive thinking or research in this area, probably because of the pressure of audit deadlines and other commitments. The general lack of sophistication of audit staff personnel within this area is also apparent: this seems to be almost universally noted. But measures are being taken to correct this situation. Staff training sessions with heavy emphasis on computers and coördination with non-computer audit procedures are also apparent. The answers to question 13 ("In your formal staff training programs how do you handle the role of computers in business systems?") indicate this rather clearly.

The second part of the questionnaire (Part B) is concerned with the more normative phase of the public accountant's work, that of system design and implementation. This is directly relevant to the auditing problems, for the system dictates the direction in which audit procedures have to be revised and restructured if the auditor is to express an opinion on the financial statements of the business firm. Accordingly, Part B was directed primarily towards the management services department of the public accounting firm. The survey responses show that there are approximately seven audit staff men for every one in the management services department. This, however, still represents a significant portion of the entire complex of the public accounting firm. Out of 447 men in the management services departments of the firms included in the survey, 169 (approximately 38 per cent) are designated as "EDP specialists." These specialists participated in 332 EDP "feasibility" studies since January 1, 1960, of which 229 (69 per cent) were implemented. During the same period, 31 tape-oriented computer systems were reviewed for possible abandonment and eight were actually abandoned.

This survey coverage certainly represents a significant portion of the computer installations in the United States today. There is little doubt that the shaping of the business system of the future will be greatly influenced by these EDP specialists in the public accounting firms. What these people consider to be the major weaknesses in existing tape-oriented computer systems is therefore significant. Their answers on this issue (question 31) follow:

Weakness or deficiency	No. of replies
Inefficient system design	15
Poor documentation of EDP system	15
Controls are too centralized	2
Lack of input-output controls	2
No economic justification	2
Poor integration with non-computer portion of system	1
Poor "software"	1
Poor use of computer output	1
Poor scheduling of computer time	1
Need for random access equipment	1

The predominant deficiency noted, the conceptual framework within which the computer operates, also appears quite prominently in the answers to a question (38) concerned with the major problems involved in the development of integrated data-processing systems:

Major problem areas	No. of replies
Competency of personnel	10
Definition of the system	8
Costs of data transmission	6
Non-acceptance on the part of management	5
Time required for design and installation	3
Control problem with input data	3
Problem of balancing system	2
Programming difficulties with in-line systems	2
Lack of flexibility of EDP system	1

Views on the problem of system design as it relates to internal control procedures (question 34) deal with various EDP procedures and techniques which are implemented primarily for the purpose of improving the effectiveness of internal control in business-oriented computer systems. Specifically, the question asks the degree of emphasis placed upon each procedure. The following results were obtained:

| Procedure | Emphasis | | | |
	Great	Moderate	Little	None
Separating duties of programmers from those of operators	16	5	1	0
Establishing an independent center for preparing data for input to computer	10	11	1	1
Separating data-processing center from accounting department	7	7	7	3

Procedure	Great	Emphasis Moderate	Little	None
Using internal auditors to strengthen internal controls on data-processing center	9	3	12	0
Use of post-audit techniques to control operation of data-processing center	5	12	4	1
Intensive use of internal and external controls on totals	1	1	0	0
Documentation of procedures	1	1	0	0

In a similar vein, a specific internal control problem was posed (question 33)—that of the possibility of the unauthorized intervention of console operators. The following suggestions were offered as a solution to this problem:

Suggestion	No. of replies
Eliminate problem of manual intervention by adoption of standard operating procedures	9
Use and control of the console log	8
Separation of duties within data-processing center	5
Utilization of internal auditors to control console operator	3
Comparison of planned time and actual operating time for a particular production run on computer	1
Programmed print-out of key-entered data	1
Surprise tests by independent auditors	1

Despite the concern over accounting-type internal control procedures, the problem of employee defalcations does not appear to be significant in the answers to question 32. Only six cases of employee defalcations were reported. Of these, four were due to punch card substitution or alteration. One was due to collusion between the key-punch operator and the console operator. The other apparently involved the unauthorized use of the computer during the night, while the regular operators were not on duty.

The final group of questions in Part B concerned the technology of computer equipment, its reliability, implementation problems, and technical deficiencies. Question 35 asks how often various problems occur in the implementation phase of the design and installation of a business-oriented computer. The results are summarized below:

Problem	Always	Usually	Some-times	Seldom	Never
Availability of qualified company personnel	4	16	0	3	0

Problem	Always	Usually	Some-times	Seldom	Never
Underestimation of equipment time requirements	o	10	o	11	1
Reliability of central processor	o	1	o	12	7
Reliability of input-output devices	o	9	2	9	2
Acceptance by managerial and supervisory personnel	2	8	1	12	o
Availability of software	2	8	2	9	1
Inadequate testing and documentation	o	2	o	o	o
Analysis of time and costs	1	1	o	o	o
Oversimplification by EDP salesmen	1	o	o	o	o
Question not applicable to office—1					

Question 36 sought views about the future of COBOL (common business-oriented language) as it relates to business data-processing programming techniques. The rather surprising results are overwhelmingly negative. Comments are summarized below:

Comment about COBOL	No. of replies
It is several years off	3
It needs to be modified	3
A common business-oriented language is impractical	2
It is limited	3
It will be replaced	3
It is not applicable to production runs	1
It is too complex	1
It looks good at present	4
It will standardize programming	1
It is useful as a bridge between systems	1

Responses to another question (37) reveal views on the present deficiencies in computer hardware in terms of suggestions for technical improvements public accounting firms would find desirable:

Recommendation to manufacturer	Level of importance		
	Primary	Great	Little
Further developments in mass-storage memory devices	8	12	5
Universal adoption of a problem-oriented language	8	11	6
Additional emphasis on data input conversion devices such as optical scanners	11	14	1
Development of higher speed peripheral equipment	6	12	7
Development of lower cost hardware	9	9	5
Development of techniques and methods which will substantially reduce installation costs	10	11	4
Solution of programming problems by means other than programming	1	o	o
Change in rentals during early months	1	o	o

It appears, then, that the management services departments of the public accounting firms are much closer to the problems of business-oriented computers than are the audit staff personnel. Their approach is constructive and should greatly enhance the chances of future success for more sophisticated data-processing systems. Perhaps the biggest disappointment to system designers is the rather gloomy outlook for the implementation of any significant developments in integrated data-processing systems. Another disappointment is the lack of familiarity with COBOL and the adverse comments made concerning its future.

Summary of Current Auditing Procedures

The approaches to the problem of auditing business-oriented computers can be classified as : (1) maintenance of conventional audit trail procedures; (2) utilization of test data with predetermined solutions to check operations of company's program; (3) use of a controlled copy of client's computer programs; and (4) use of a computerized audit program in place of conventional methods. In addition to these four basic classifications, there appears to be rather general agreement that greater emphasis must be placed on procedure reviews, on internal and external data control, and in some cases on increased use of statistical methods.

The maintenance of conventional audit trail procedures is supported by all the early articles, by the standard textbooks in the field, and by the answers to the survey questionnaire. The advantages and disadvantages of this method can be summarized as follows:

Advantages:

(1) Procedures are readily understood by all audit staff personnel.

(2) This approach lends itself to batch-controlled installations which form the predominant portion of current business-oriented computer installations.

Disadvantages:

(1) This method is extremely costly in terms of computer time.

(2) It tends to inhibit development of integrated data-processing systems.

(3) The auditor gains no benefit from the computer.

The utilization of test data with predetermined solutions as a method of checking the operation of the client's computer program is the second most popular approach according to the survey, and it has been discussed favorably in the literature. It possesses certain advantages over the maintenance of conventional audit trail methods, but it is necessary also to consider its disadvantages.

Advantages:

(1) The procedures are readily understood by personnel and do not require a high level of sophistication with computer techniques and procedures.

(2) The results can be easily checked.

(3) It eliminates or at least substantially reduces the need for conventional audit trail techniques.

Disadvantages:

(1) This is of limited applicability to the auditing of sophisticated systems since integrated data-processing systems cannot be tested by this method.

(2) It requires different sets of data for different systems. Therefore it may be excessively costly in terms of audit time.

(3) The auditor is unable to satisfy himself that the program tested was the one which was, in fact, actually used during the test period.

The use of a controlled copy of the client's computer program has several advantages over the previously described methods. If this approach is used, however, someone familiar with computer programming must carefully review the client's detailed program together with the flow charts and block diagrams in order to assure the auditor that the program as written will perform according to plan. The easiest way this can be accomplished is for the auditor to participate in the feasibility and implementation phases of the installation of the client's computer. The alternative of reviewing an existing computer program is more difficult but not excessively costly in terms of time or effort. Once the public accounting firm is satisfied that the program, as written, is satisfactory, other advantages and disadvantages must be considered.

Advantages:

(1) It eliminates the need for the public accounting firm to write its own program.

(2) It takes advantage of the company's specialized knowledge of the peculiarities of its EDP system.

(3) It eliminates the need for audit trail requirements.

Disadvantages:

(1) It requires separate programs for each client.

(2) It requires a method of updating programs for changes instituted by the client during the period from one year to the next.

(3) When a client changes auditors this means that an undue amount of time must be devoted by the new auditors to a review of the computer program.

The use of a computerized audit program written independently by the public accounting firm does not seem to have received very wide acceptance in the review of client computer procedures. There is one reference to this approach in the literature and only one comment in the responses to the questionnaire inquiry. Nowhere is there any thought of developing such a program in a generalized sense. Even Toan's article assumes that such a program would be written for one specific client. One of the reasons for this situation is the failure to think in terms of a common problem-oriented language. Given such a common language (COBOL or FORTRAN),[13] it would be at least tentatively feasible to develop a general program for use on a variety of computers. Such a program would be completely independent of the program of any particular client. Audit trails could be largely dispensed with since only the basic input data would be used. All connecting links between the input and output would be incorporated into the auditor's computerized program. But this approach possesses disadvantages, too. The advantages and disadvantages can be summarized as follows:

Advantages:

(1) The independent attitude of the auditor is preserved.

(2) It is useful in many situations and need not be tailor-made to a particular client's system.

(3) After initial development, the program may actually reduce the time necessary to test the system of internal control, allowing the auditor to take advantage of the computer.

Disadvantages:

(1) Requires the use of a common programming language (if prohibitive costs are to be avoided).

(2) Requires that client's input data be available in machine-sensible form to convert for use in audit program.

(3) Requires flexibility in computerized audit program in order to be useful in different types of installations.

The implications of this approach are explored more fully in chapter vi. As we have seen, the accounting functions most usually processed on tape-oriented computers are payrolls, billing and accounts receivable, and inventories. Accordingly, we will discuss two models, a generalized application for review of a computerized payroll system, and a combined order, billing, accounts receivable and inventory model.

---

[13] COBOL is the accepted abbreviation for "Common Business-Oriented Language" developed by the CODASYL Committee in 1960. FORTRAN is the accepted abbreviation for "Formula Translation," a language adaptable to scientific or business applications, developed by Bell Laboratories and IBM in 1956.

VI

Auditing "Through The Computer"

The survey findings reported in chapter v reinforce the view that the public accounting profession has tended to view the computer as an obstacle to be overcome before an opinion can be expressed regarding the financial statements of the client. We have focused so far on the auditor's function vis-à-vis the client's EDP system. Now we turn to a further aspect of computer data processing as it relates to the auditor's function—an approach which utilizes the power of the computer as an aid in performing some of the audit procedures themselves. It is not unreasonable at least to consider it likely that if the methodology of review were technically compatible with the methodology of what is being reviewed many of the problems of auditing EDP business information would become less acute. Indeed, the auditor's resistance to computerizing client operations would doubtless disappear, and he would assume greater responsibility and initiative in encouraging clients to use EDP procedures more extensively and more effectively.

In order to appreciate the potentials of this aspect of the EDP-as-related-to-auditing situation, a shift of perspective is in order. When the auditor reviews a system of internal control, he takes the following steps:

(1) He establishes a clear view of the needs presumably to be met by the system—its ideal objectives. The ultimate evaluation of the system rests on how it measures up to this criterion. (To be sure, the auditor may not explicitly take this step in each engagement, for "becoming an auditor" to a large extent is a matter of doing just this. But the specific situation may commend explicit attention in this area.)

(2) He reviews the conceptual framework of the particular system of the accounting and administrative controls actually employed by the client in processing business data; that is, he analyzes the design of the client's system as revealed by an internal control questionnaire, discus-

sions with operating personnel, and study of organization manuals and charts—and compares it with his conceptualization of the system ideally.

(3) He then evaluates the functional sufficiency of the system by testing the actual operation, using the client's raw input data as a starting point for determining the validity of the client's conclusions as represented by summaries, general ledger totals, and operating reports.

(4) Based on the results of this test, usually performed by the junior members of the audit staff, the accountant in charge determines the extent to which additional tests of the system of internal control must be made and to what extent subsequent audit procedures must be modified.

Utilized effectively in this review of the system of internal control, the computer can to a large extent replace the junior staff member who traditionally performs the test of transactions referred to in Step 3. The junior staff member implicitly has in mind a basic system he considers acceptable and against which he measures the effectiveness of the client's operational system. The second phase of his work involves the actual mechanical computations and comparisons necessary to test the operational system. The final step is to compare the tests results with the historical averages of errors which the auditor has recorded from his earlier reviews of the system of internal control; or, in the absence of an acceptable historical norm, the auditor sets a norm based upon his preliminary analysis of the client's EDP system.

If the computer is to replace or assist the junior staff member in performing the test of transactions, it must be fed detailed instructions. Hence, the senior accountant must be competent to provide a computer program which will perform the tests or portions of them. Since the computer has neither ingenuity nor humor, the program must cover every possible contingency in prosaic, straightforward, detailed instructions. According to the results of the survey reported in chapter v, most supervising accountants are not capable of preparing such a computer program. On the other hand, the survey also shows that if a sufficiently general program could be developed for application in several engagements of similar scope, it might be utilized by the in-charge accountants. The coöperation of the management services department or outside consultants might assist in developing such a program. But it is important for the audit staff to have the primary responsibility for the development of the computer audit program, for the auditing perspective of the problem must prevail.

In formulating this perspective, it is helpful, as indicated in step 1, to construct an ideal system—a model—for the particular accounting function or segment of the data-processing system under review. Then, using the client's original input data, the auditor can compare the client's output against the output which results from using the ideal system to process the original data. Programmed to follow the principle of exception reporting, the scheme can generate computer output which records only the deviations from the theoretical ideal system. Then, using a sequential sampling technique, the computer program can also generate tentative conclusions. These may comprise a sufficient basis for the supervising auditor's decision as to the effectiveness of the client's computer programs and data-processing system.

Payroll Model

The sample payroll model which follows is conceived as an ideal payroll processing system against which the actual system employed by the client can be tested. The model generates a tentative conclusion; but it remains for the supervising auditor to determine whether the client's system is acceptable by professional standards.

The ideal model would review the business information system in its entirety. General principles applicable to development of a more inclusive model for reviewing a partially integrated data-processing system will be illustrated in the second half of this chapter, where the order-billing procedure—including the record-keeping functions involved in accounts receivable, and the related effects on inventory balances—is considered.

Payrolls are usually processed by using a batching technique. Figure 2 illustrates the process of updating the master file during the payroll processing operation.

Construction of a sample payroll model requires making several assumptions about the type of files maintained in machine-sensible form. In an actual situation these assumptions would be supplanted by knowledge of the files actually kept. The following files were assumed to be available to the auditor, either on magnetic tape or on punched cards:

(1) Master payroll file (end of test period—last year.)
(2) Master payroll file (beginning of test period—this year.)
(3) Master payroll file (end of test period—this year.)
(4) Detail record file of time cards for test period.
(5) Social security quarterly tax report.
(6) Payroll check file for test period.
(7) Labor distribution summary file for test period.
A basic batch-controlled EDP system is illustrated in figure 2. Since the

model payroll program development and testing was limited to equipment for which files were prepared on punched cards and processed as indicated in figure 3, some adjustment to the basic batch-controlled technique was necessary.

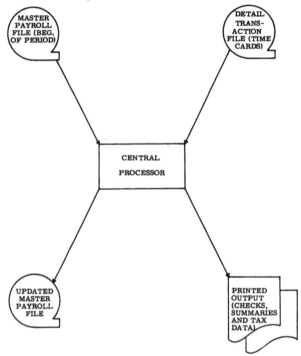

Fig. 2. A simplified batch-controlled payroll application.

The basic program for the audit of payroll records is outlined in Holmes:[1]

1. Review the system of internal control.
2. Inspect employment records.
3. Compare payroll with cash disbursed.
4. Test computations of individual earnings.
5. Test hours and rates.
6. Test payroll record footings, posting, and distributions.
7. Compare individual checks with individual earnings.
8. Reconcile the total payroll with federal data.
9. Examine bonus plans and pension plans.
10. Verify unclaimed wages.
11. Verify accrued wages and salaries.
12. Attend or perform a distribution of the payroll.

[1] Arthur W. Holmes, *Auditing, Principles and Procedures* (Homewood, Ill.: Richard D. Irwin, 1959), p. 714.

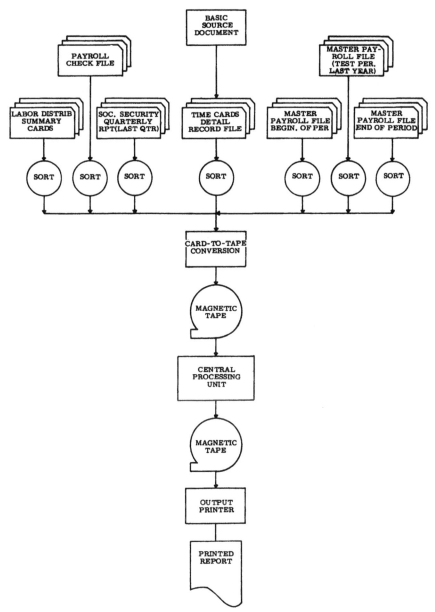

Fig. 3. Configuration of processing equipment.

The payroll model which was constructed performs steps 1-8, leaving the remaining four steps to be executed in the normal manner by audit staff personnel. Although it would be possible to extend the payroll model to cover step 11, steps 9, 10, and 12 could not be incorporated into the computer program.

The basic logic of the payroll programs is outlined in figure 4. The first step involves the matching of the detail time records with the master payroll record. The individual employee's data are then processed through a series of tests as indicated. When the tests for one employee are completed, the program returns control to the matching routine and selects the next employee for test. Whenever an exception appears for an individual employee, the appropriate notation is made on the output tape, and a statistical test, subroutine STTEST, is applied in order to determine whether a decision can be made as to whether the sample should be accepted or rejected. This decision depends on the size of the sample and the number of times the exception occurs.

When all employees in the test period have been processed subroutine OVRVEW applies; this summarizes the results of the test period review. A recapitulation of the results integrates the exception number findings with the statistical decisions made with regard to each exception. The sequential sampling decision rules used here in subroutine STTEST were adapted from Cyert and Davidson's *Statistical Sampling for Accounting Information*.[2] The block diagrams for the payroll program appear in Appendix B. The detail FORTRAN programs, together with the sample output, are also included.

This model has some characteristics which are significantly different from models discussed in the literature:

(1) Constructed as an ideal system, the model seeks to measure significant variances from the actual system in use by the client.

(2) It provides for limited computer decision making on acceptance or rejection of a client's program (here payroll only).

(3) It allows for use of a sequential sampling technique when the results are indeterminate, possibly permitting an accept or reject decision after additional testing.

(4) It is completely general in the sense that it is not oriented toward any one payroll system and is written in a problem-oriented language.

(5) Quantitative data consistent with the client's output are suppressed; only exceptions and related quantitative statistical interpretations are reported.

---

[2] R. M. Cyert and H. Justin Davidson, *Statistical Sampling for Accounting Information* (Englewood Cliffs, N.J.: Prentice-Hall, Inc., 1962), pp. 163-165.

KEY

1. IS TIME CARD MISSING?
2. WAS EMPLOYE TERMINATED?
3. WAS EMPLOYE PAID?
4. WAS EMPLOYE ON VACATION?
5. WAS EMPLOYE ON SICK LEAVE?
6. IS MASTER CARD MISSING?
7. WAS EMPLOYE PAID?
8. WAS EMPLOYE IN TEST PERIOD LAST YEAR?
9. IS EMPLOYE IN WRONG DEPARTMENT?
10. ARE EMPLOYE'S HOURS IN EXCESS OF 40?
11. ARE EMPLOYE'S HOURS IN EXCESS OF 44?
12. IS IDLE TIME IN EXCESS OF 5%?
13. IS EMPLOYE'S RATE IN EXCESS OF UNION RATE?
14. ARE EMPLOYE'S TAXABLE WAGES OVER $4,800?
15. IS EMPLOYE ON FICA RETURN?
16. IS HIRING PRIOR TO ENDING DATE OF FICA RETURN?
17. IS EMPLOYE NEW SINCE LAST YEAR?
18. WAS EMPLOYE HIRED THIS YEAR ACCORDING TO MASTER PERSONNEL
19. ARE ALL TIME CARDS DISTRIBUTED?   FILE?
20. IS ERROR IN EXCESS OF 5%?
21. WAS EMPLOYE PAID?
22. WAS HE PAID RIGHT AMOUNT?
23. IS ERROR IN EXCESS OF 5%?

E   INDICATES EXCEPTION TO BE RECORDED.

A   INDICATES ACCEPTANCE WITHOUT EXCEPTION

R   SIGNIFIES END OF TEST SINCE EMPLOYE DID NOT WORK AND WAS NOT
     PAID FOR TEST PERIOD.

X   SIGNIFIES END OF TEST SINCE EMPLOYE WAS ON VACATION OR SICK LEAVE.

Fig. 4. Sequential decision process for evaluating the system of internal control relating to payrolls.

(6) Being independent of a specific client program, the model program meets the criteria specified for audit programs generally. The compatibility of format specifications still remains, however, as a technical problem. (As a partial solution, a variable format feature could be incorporated in a working program, so that any configuration of data could be made compatible with the reading of a format control card.)

(7) It is simple and readily grasped in terms of the logic of the sequential decision-making process.

(8) The model program highlights the essential characteristics of a payroll audit program and allows flexibility in implementation through the use of subroutines.

(9) Through its emphasis on the "flow" concept, it provides a stepping stone toward the consideration of audit programs applicable to integrated data-processing systems.

The model's parameters, which are used by way of illustration only, merit some consideration. Each auditor using a model program might have his own opinion as to the relative weights to be assigned to the deviations from the norm, and would indicate these prior to running the program. Having to do this encourages the human auditor to think relatively about deviations and the significance of each, a crucial professional function. Thus, the computerized audit program, rather than removing the opportunity for the exercise of professional judgment, highlights the need for such judgment. The need is similar with problems in selecting confidence levels for use when applying statistical sampling techniques in computerized auditing.[3]

The use of this payroll model does not exclude the need for verification of primary source data fed to the system. Virtually all authorities agree that such verification must take place. The illustrative validity checks on primary source data incorporated into the payroll model do not entirely eliminate the need for human verification of source data, however. The only currently conceivable way in which independent verification may be eliminated would be through interchange of intercompany data among accounting firms. At the present time such an arrangement is not feasible. But perhaps the increased use of business-oriented computers will encourage development of a master information retrieval system which will eliminate, or at least substantially reduce, independent verification.

---

[3] Lawrence L. Vance, "A Review of Developments in Statistical Sampling for Accountants," *Accounting Review,* XXXV (January, 1960), 19-28.

ORDER-PROCESSING MODEL

The basic distinction between a batch-controlled system and an in-line system is the method by which files are updated and maintained. From the audit standpoint, the basic concern with in-line systems arises because any file updating results in the destruction of the previous information; the detail of the individual transactions (sometimes referred to as intermediate processing) is not retained in the system after the account balances are updated. A simplified model of an in-line system is shown in figure 5. The detail block diagrams and computer program are given in Appendix C.

The classic discussion of in-line accounting and audit trail by Price Waterhouse for IBM in 1958[4] specifies three basic areas of interest in which the accountant is involved: (1) underlying documents, (2) transaction analysis, and (3) balances. While the underlying documents themselves may be available, they do not *per se* form a part of the computer system, but must be converted to machine-sensible form, and this input data typically appears in chronological order. In the standard configuration of in-line systems, balances, too, are available at specified intervals. Whether they exist in the form of hard-copy output or are converted to punched cards or magnetic tape for off-line printing is a matter of individual system design. This model assumes that the client maintains the details of periodic reports in punched-card form. This is probably the typical situation; it does not impose an undue restriction. However, the details of the transactions during the period under review are lacking, and the audit trail does not exist. If the periodic report details are not maintained in machine-sensible form, the information can readily be obtained from hard-copy reports.

The Price Waterhouse report suggests that the most direct means of providing an audit trail is to have the system produce a punched card with the details of every transaction processed. But it goes on to point out that this method has two disadvantages: (1) In most cases it adds significantly to the operations necessary for processing the data, and places a heavy added burden on the output facilities of the system and reduces its efficiency. (2) It also requires that manual or tabulating card files be maintained in addition to the information stored internally and the other supporting data available. This method is certainly not appropriate in most installations. An alternative, which is not discussed by Price Waterhouse, is illustrated in the present model.

---

[4] International Business Machines Corporation, *In-Line Electronic Accounting, Internal Control and Audit Trail*, General Information Manual (New York: IBM Corporation, 1958), p. 7.

Input data should be similar in most respects to transaction data. There are circumstances in which the two differ, however, and an adjustment is needed. If, for example, the input data consists of a customer's purchase order, this information must be converted to transaction data during the processing. The following differences might occur:

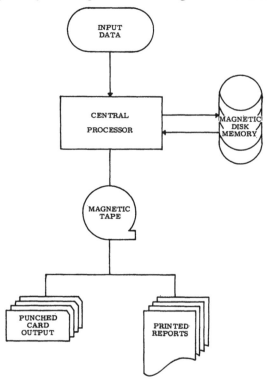

Fig. 5. A simplified in-line accounting system.

(1) differences in quantity between what the customer ordered and the amount shipped and billed to the customer, possibly resulting from stock-outs on merchandise ordered, limitations imposed by customer credit limits, or inability to comply with terms of order as to shipping dates, specifications, etc; (2) price differentials resulting from incorrect purchase order prices or subsequent changes in company policies; (3) standard or historical cost prices not, in the normal situation, shown on the purchase order. Such information can be stored on a disk file and entered as a part of the transaction record at the time an order is processed.

It is theoretically possible to start with the input data in machine-sensible form and, with an ideally structured program, to reprocess the client's data during the period under review and compare the test results with those found in the client's output. This could be done, if sufficient random-access equipment is available, by reprocessing input data in a manner identical to that used by the client in accumulating his ending balances. Otherwise, the in-line process can be approximated by using a batch-controlled technique to review the in-line system. Generally, random-access equipment is (or should be) reasonably well loaded and the auditor should not depend on being given sufficient storage space to process a period's transactions. In the typical situation, some aspects of the computer system will be made available to the auditor, most frequently input-output equipment, tape units, and the central processor and internal core storage normally available to the central processor. The model discussed here uses a batch-controlled technique.

As with the payroll model, the order-processing model rests on several assumptions about the "real life" situation. (These assumptions in no way affect the logical structure of the model.) They may be briefly stated as follows: (1) No incoming shipments of merchandise are received during the test period. (2) The tests of credits to accounts receivable (cash receipts or returned merchandise) are not considered to be a part of the basic input data. (3) There are no outstanding orders for merchandise at the beginning of the test period. (4) Shipments are assumed to be made the same day the orders are received (unless the item must be back-ordered).

Again as with the earlier model, the auditor must still perform various additional checks independently of the computer audit program, particularly in two important areas: (1) He must separately check the validity of the input data. (2) He must also obtain a print-out of selected inventory items and review them for proper costing information. This is essential to insure proper processing of dollar inventory balances and proper recording of costs.

The standard audit program as outlined by Holmes was used as the basis of testing the completeness of the model. Holmes lists 22 general audit procedures for the examination of revenues.[5] Only the first eleven are applicable to this model: the latter eleven refer to types of revenue accounts or to sales returns or cash receipts transactions not considered to be an integral part of the model program. The relevant eleven steps are:

(1) Verify revenues through the audit of the original records.
(2) Investigate the system of internal control.
(3) Audit by comparison.

---

[5] Holmes, *op. cit.*, p. 693.

(4) Compare invoice prices with price lists.
(5) Verify extensions, footings, and discounts.
(6) Trace sales from invoices to the sales records.
(7) Foot sales records.
(8) Trace sales record postings to the general ledger accounts.
(9) Verify postings to customers' accounts.
(10) Verify postings to inventory accounts.
(11) Examine and compare sales and shipping records.

The computer audit program covers all of these points with the exception (since cash receipts are, by assumption, not included in the model) of testing discounts (point 5). If the input data are received in machine-sensible form and it is necessary to verify independently that all unit records are supported by bona fide sales orders received from the customers, this is done manually. All other audit procedures are satisfied by the method outlined on the following pages.

The configuration of the processing equipment is given in figure 6. The approach taken in this model varies somewhat from the payroll model described earlier. In the payroll model, the review covered each employee's data for all aspects of conformance to the acceptable standard before proceeding to the next employee. This second model provides for processing all orders for a particular exception before proceeding to the next test. Consequently, the arrangement of the output differs, too. The payroll model recorded all exceptions for a particular employee sequentially; the order-processing model, emphasizing the functioning of particular segments of the client's computer program, groups output by those segments. In both models, however, the summary of the exceptions is identical; so, too, are the statistical conclusions, both as to arrangement of the data and the method of testing the conclusions. By and large, then, the models take substantially the same approach and demonstrate, from an audit standpoint, the similarity of batch-controlled and in-line systems. Neither model requires the maintenance of a continuous audit trail for the benefit of the auditor.

In order to construct the order-processing model, it was also necessary again to make some assumptions concerning the types of files maintained in machine-sensible form. An in-line system assumes periodic "dumping" of account balances; this dump could be in the form of magnetic tape, punched cards, or hard-copy prints-outs. The model assumes that the following files are dumped at the beginning and end of the test period:

(1) Master inventory file (beginning of test period.)
(2) Master inventory file (end of test period.)
(3) General ledger control totals (beginning and end of test period.)

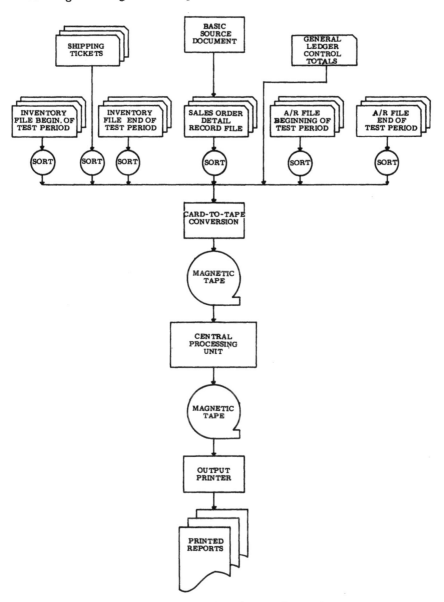

Fig. 6. Configuration of processing equipment.

(4) Accounts receivable file (beginning of test period.)

(5) Accounts receivable file (end of test period.)

The model also assumes that the client has maintained chronological listings of shipping tickets and of sales orders. The key document is the sales order. Before running the computer audit program, the validity of the sales order must be independently verified as to its terms and authenticity. Given the validity of the sales order, the system can be tested by the model. Some validity checks might be incorporated into the audit program; this would reduce, but would not eliminate, the need for independent verification of the sales order as a necessary condition of successful utilization of the computer to contribute to the auditing function.

Because of the exception noted above, the sequential decision process for evaluating the system of internal control relating to order-processing, as shown in figure 7, is presented in a slightly different format from the payroll model. A word of explanation is in order regarding the exceptions which are considered important in the order-processing model. Since, by assumption, there are no outstanding orders for merchandise at the beginning of the test period, a case in which shipments exceed orders should not be possible; if one appears, it gives rise to an Exception No. 2 entry. A shipment not backed up by a bona-fide shipping order would also be tagged as unauthorized. If shipping orders exceed shipments, or if unshipped orders exist, the ending inventory record should provide a backorder quantity. If the system is working properly, the total number of Exceptions No. 3 and No. 4 should equal the total backorder discrepancies listed under Exception No. 7. In the hypothetical data used to test the program, this is indeed the case.

The computer programs presented in this chapter are illustrative only. The discussion has assumed that some problem-oriented language compatible with almost all popular business-oriented computers is essential to the implementation of these models. As a matter of expediency, since this was the only suitable problem-oriented language available at the University of California Computer Center, these programs were written in FORTRAN; but FORTRAN is not necessarily the best language conceivable for the purpose. As a matter of fact, the input-output conventions inherent in FORTRAN are not readily adaptable to the format conventions of many individual installations. This constitutes a serious flaw in the use of FORTRAN.

The only other current programming language useful in this context is COBOL. But COBOL, too, raises some difficulties. The survey responses about COBOL (see chapter v) indicate that it is not uni-

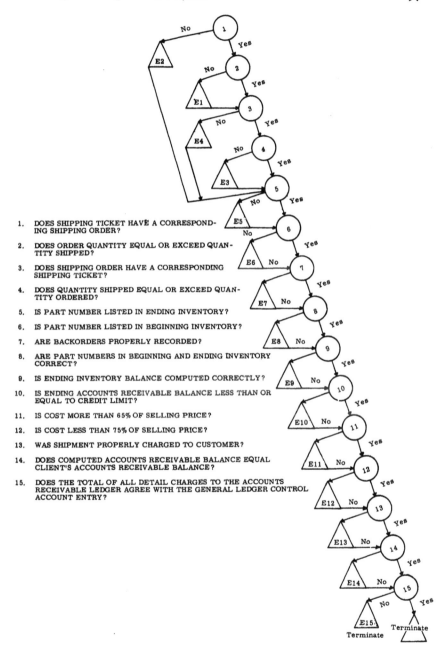

1. DOES SHIPPING TICKET HAVE A CORRESPONDING SHIPPING ORDER?

2. DOES ORDER QUANTITY EQUAL OR EXCEED QUANTITY SHIPPED?

3. DOES SHIPPING ORDER HAVE A CORRESPONDING SHIPPING TICKET?

4. DOES QUANTITY SHIPPED EQUAL OR EXCEED QUANTITY ORDERED?

5. IS PART NUMBER LISTED IN ENDING INVENTORY?

6. IS PART NUMBER LISTED IN BEGINNING INVENTORY?

7. ARE BACKORDERS PROPERLY RECORDED?

8. ARE PART NUMBERS IN BEGINNING AND ENDING INVENTORY CORRECT?

9. IS ENDING INVENTORY BALANCE COMPUTED CORRECTLY?

10. IS ENDING ACCOUNTS RECEIVABLE BALANCE LESS THAN OR EQUAL TO CREDIT LIMIT?

11. IS COST MORE THAN 65% OF SELLING PRICE?

12. IS COST LESS THAN 75% OF SELLING PRICE?

13. WAS SHIPMENT PROPERLY CHARGED TO CUSTOMER?

14. DOES COMPUTED ACCOUNTS RECEIVABLE BALANCE EQUAL CLIENT'S ACCOUNTS RECEIVABLE BALANCE?

15. DOES THE TOTAL OF ALL DETAIL CHARGES TO THE ACCOUNTS RECEIVABLE LEDGER AGREE WITH THE GENERAL LEDGER CONTROL ACCOUNT ENTRY?

Fig. 7. Sequential decision process for evaluating the system of internal control relating to order-processing for an in-line accounting system.

versally acceptable at the present time. However, this need not deter the auditor from taking advantage of it. COBOL was designed expressly for the purpose of providing a bridge between computers of various manufacturers, and it would seem, therefore, to be more suitable for use in connection with the computer audit programs described in this chapter. However, the problems of format conventions should not be minimized; there may be serious problems with individual installations, at least during the first year of operation, and these problems require the services of the management services department, with its superior knowledge of computer programming, in order to adapt the program to a particular installation.

Various simplifying assumptions made in connection with both the models may not be realistic in some real-life situations. This does not detract from the value of models, but emphasizes the importance of adapting an audit program to fit the peculiar circumstances of individual installations. The need for modification is particularly likely in connection with the order-processing model. And truly general models may well emerge as the more particular models, subjected to extensive testing in practice, are revised to include more built-in contingency factors and thereby achieve greater flexibility.

In addition to the format specifications of particular data-processing installations and the limited generality in these models, the statistical parameters are of crucial importance. If they are to be built into the program, the auditor must determine *in advance* both the confidence levels for testing sequential sampling decision rules and the percentage of errors he will consider acceptable in a given set of circumstances. Auditors may tend to resist giving up the prerogative of making these decisions in each individual case in the light of the circumstances arising *after* the test is completed. In effect, this problem is already evident in the auditor's reluctance to accept sampling rules proposed in the literature. Other parameters also become important, such as the percentage of idle computer time to be considered circumstantially normal and the percentage of distribution error tolerable in a given situation. However, these problems seem to be less worrisome, for the average data-processing installation does not turn up a great number of errors in any area. They can be viewed as requiring a simple "Go/No-Go" decision. Either the computer program as structured by the client is working or it is not.

VII

The Future Of The Business-Oriented Computer And Its Impact On Auditing Theory And Practice

The central problem the public accounting profession must solve in auditing business information systems that use business-oriented computers arises from the greater or lesser obliteration of the audit trail. It is not surprising that a profession which for six decades has been able to follow the transformation from verifiable, objective inputs to predictable outputs should attempt to retain a method which is easily understandable, which leads to definitive results with a minimum of ambiguity, and which has been accepted by government agencies, the investing public, and the majority of the writers in the field. But this very insistence on maintaining the status quo inhibits technological progress, and even optimal application of already-developed technology, in the field of EDP business information systems. To be sure, auditors must be satisfied, must feel and be firmly in control of their work. If this is possible only if they limit the computer to recording transactions in a manner similar to manual methods, and to serving as a computative device with an extremely efficient output mechanism, then the profession is going to deprive itself of vast potentials for leadership in the business community. Perhaps even worse, as business advances its records technology without that leadership, the auditing profession may well find itself hard pressed to keep abreast.

It is significant that the Auditing Procedures Committee has made no official statement on the problems involved in auditing a business firm that uses the business-oriented computer for data processing. This silence can hardly be justified on grounds of the recency of such usage. Ten years have allowed for enormous technological progress. Ten years have permitted the business information system trend to become abundantly clear. Ten years have made the needs for auditing innovation all but imperative. Ten years have made the opportunity more than evident.

Fortunately, some developments in auditing theory, apart from any influence of the business-oriented computer, have been fortuitously compatible with the technological progress. Increasing emphasis on the review of accounting and administrative controls as they relate to the data-processing systems, or more generally to the business information system of the firm, has developed for other reasons, largely because of the increasing volume and complexity of records. To some extent change has been prompted by having to deal with the problem of seasonal peaks, a problem which can be met only by some form of "real-time" auditing. The idea that a greater portion of the audit is advantageously performed prior to the year-end date has gained more and more acceptance during the past fifteen years. The business-oriented computer naturally fits into this pattern. However, it is clear that the profession has not adequately recognized this—at least the literature and the practitioners' behavior do not, by and large, indicate much recognition.

Indeed, designers of computer systems must be free to express *their* ingenuity to the fullest, to program the computer in the most efficient way possible. Their concern, quite properly, must emphasize external requirements which are essential to the operation of the system. But to respect the freedom of the systems designer is not *ipso facto* an abdication of the auditor's responsibility for reviewing the system. It is, indeed, an assumption of responsibility to adapt old procedures and techniques, and to devise new ones for an adequate review.

New procedures and techniques might take several forms that are not mutually exclusive, such as: (1) review of internal and external controls on the computer system itself; (2) a use of test data to review the operation of the computer program; and (3) an audit program which itself utilizes the computer. It was quite clear from the questionnaire responses reviewed in chapter v that the first approach has already been rather widely accepted by the public accounting profession. It is compatible with the maintenance of audit trails and is not avoidable when audit procedure simply must deal with information maintained by computer.

The second also enjoys a limited amount of acceptance, and for much the same reasons. However, there is a serious problem here. It has not been adequately discussed in the literature; nor did the survey responses seem to appreciate its significance. As we have seen, procedures and techniques used to audit EDP operations must include assumptions about the type of system being considered; they must take into account the peculiarities of form and content of the data under review (this is, indeed, almost the definition of the review phase of auditing—an "accounting of accounting"). There is a fundamental difference between batch-controlled systems and in-line systems, for example. This difference must be borne in mind in considering audit procedures to be applied in particular installations. As a matter of fact, the literature has in large measure failed to consider this key distinction, and with much consequent confusion. To be sure, audit trail, properly implemented, provides a solution in either case, but it makes for excessive cost and delay—and to a large extent unnecessarily. In failing to take advantage of the computer, in sticking to traditional data and "look-up" procedures, the auditor demonstrates at best a formal conservatism—not necessarily a functional competence.

Review of internal and external controls is definitely needed, but this procedure certainly is not sufficient. The use of test decks may well be appropriate to some types of batch-controlled installations, but their use for in-line systems is problematical. The more fully integrated the computer system, the more complex are the problems of using test decks for reviewing operations.

The computerized audit programs developed in this study may be adapted to either batch-controlled or in-line systems. But since the models are simple, they are not adaptable to the more complex on-line, real-time systems. However, a more generalized model can be made for use in integrated data-processing systems. As has been noted, development of a more generalized computer audit requires extensive testing and review of variants of the simpler models. Once the applicability of various alternatives is known and the conditions relating to statistical methodology have been clarified, detailed study of more generalized models should be highly rewarding. The public accounting profession still has time for exploratory study and testing in this area, for there are no truly integrated data-processing systems in use today. Sprague has predicted that by 1970, however, nearly all accounting systems will be of the on-line, real-time variety.[1] He may be over-optimistic as to the timing of these developments, but, give or take five or ten years, the prospect is certain to materialize.

---

[1] Richard E. Sprague, *Electronic Business Systems* (New York: Ronald Press, 1962), p. iv.

THE BUSINESS INFORMATION SYSTEM:
WHERE IS IT HEADED?

The future of the business-oriented computer hinges on three factors: (1) the developing concept of the business information system, (2) technological developments, and (3) the impact of technology on auditing theory and practice. The literature is just beginning to deal with the broad concept of a business information system[2]—the problems and implications are increasingly evident. But discussion at the conceptual level enables only the broad frame of reference to be established. One cannot merely say that a business information system is concerned with the interaction of the various functional areas of business, such as marketing, production, and finance; constructive discussion demands specifying requirements for each area. Nor is it useful to discuss business information systems merely from the standpoint of the given inputs and outputs which accountants traditionally have assumed to be important.

Apart from the theoretical considerations involved in inputs, outputs, and transformation mechanisms, it is necessary to consider the direction in which the concept of integrated data-processing systems may grow. The present state of data-processing technology of business firms in the United States can be represented as a spectrum with the following bands:

(1) Traditional configurations: maintenance of hand-posted records.

(2) Bookkeeping machine systems: use of combination typewriter-adding machines for simultaneous recording of transactions and preparation of original source data.

(3) Punch card procedures: utilization of unit records to facilitate classification of data.

(4) Computer operations: machine coverage of work previously done manually.

(5) Integrated data-processing systems: implementation of the concept of point-of-occurrence recording and automatic processing of data.

(6) Sophisticated arrangements: optimal application of data collection and transmission equipment.

---

[2] See, for example, Hector R. Anton, "Activity Analysis of the Firm," *Liiketaloudellinen Aikakauskirja*, No. IV (1961), 290-305; "A Steel Company's Date with a Data Machine," *Business Week*, May 4, 1963, pp. 142-146; R. E. Pfenning, "Business Information Systems," *The Accounting Review*, XXXVII (April, 1962), 234-243; W. S. Boutell, "Business-Oriented Computers: A Frame of Reference," *The Accounting Review*, XXXIX (April, 1964), 305-311.

Roughly 25 per cent of the business firms engaging the auditors in the survey reported in chapter v fall into categories 1 and 2, 52 per cent into category 3, some 15 per cent into 4, and the remaining 8 per cent into categories 5 and 6. Since the survey design over-represents EDP-oriented auditors and their EDP clients, the national incidence of firms near the upper end of the continuum is certainly even smaller than in the survey sample. Doubtless the national distribution in categories 3 and 4 is far smaller than the two-thirds in the sample; but it may be reasonably assumed to be significant. Thus the important point in this development spectrum is the disappearance—even at levels 3 and 4—from the data-processing system *per se* of the traditional source documents on which the system still heavily depends for raw data.

Input source documents can be classified as those used for external communication (A and B in table 4) and those used for intra-firm communication (C). As data collection and transmission equipment become clearly understood and more readily available, the internally generated source documents tend to disappear first. But it increasingly seems possible that compatible technologies of direct inter-firm communication between computer systems will increasingly supplant sales invoices and purchase orders. Indeed, banking has already made notable strides in EDP external functions.

The survey indicates that even progressive auditors have serious objections to integrated data-processing systems. Economic considerations as well as a lack of education on the part of business managers are indeed consequential obstacles. But less than a decade is a rather short span of time for overcoming them. In any case, there seems little doubt about the trend; to set 1980 as a "deadline" for achieving the final phase of system development may not be unrealistic.

TECHNOLOGICAL CONSIDERATIONS

The state of purely technical development of the computer—its competence as a piece of equipment—appears, as of the mid-sixties, to be adequate for the mid-sixties' needs of business data processing. Internal speeds, consistency, reliability, and economic efficiency are relatively satisfactory. As was observed earlier, the trend toward purchase of central processors apparently reflects confidence that central processor technology will remain essentially at its present level for a period of five to ten years.[3]

Peripheral equipment presents an entirely différent situation. Origi-

---

[3] "Growing Market in Used Computers," *Business Week,* September 8, 1962, pp. 49-51. But see the announcement of IBM System/360 dated April 7, 1964.

TABLE 4

THE IMPACT OF THE COMPUTER
ON BUSINESS INFORMATION PROCESSING

Document or summary	Source or purpose	Traditional configuration	Bookkeeping machine system
Purchase Invoice Cash Receipts	Received from other business firms	Original form	Original form
Cash Disbursements Sales Inv.	Sent to other business firms	Original form	Original form
Receiving Report Time Cards	Internally generated documents	Original form	Original form
Books of Original Entry	Chronological recording of source data	Hand posted	Prepared by machine
Summary Ledgers	Data organization	Hand posted	Prepared by machine
Managerial Reports	Data for decision making	Manually prepared	Manually prepared
Financial Reports	Information for investors	Manually prepared	Manually prepared

nally, peripheral equipment was developed without regard to the requirements of business data processing, and the systems designer approaching the problems of designing an integrated system assumed that technology would remain fixed. Only very recently has the industry shown an encouraging awareness that future developments in the technology of data collection and transmission equipment must be governed in large measure by the demands of the business community. In effect, then, technological developments in peripheral equipment may well depend on how the auditing profession helps shape the wants of the business community.

Basically, the complaints of systems designers seem to center around economic considerations and lack of standardization of components. The problems of computer hardware do not seem to constitute a major stumbling block to the development of integrated EDP systems, but software problems are of crucial importance. The three problem areas of software involve problem-oriented languages, the development of standardized programs, and information retrieval.

TABLE 4

THE IMPACT OF THE COMPUTER
ON BUSINESS INFORMATION PROCESSING

Unit record machine system	Batch-controlled computer system	In-line computer system	On-line, real-time computer system 1980 A.D. (?)
Original form	Original form	Original form	Computer-to-computer communication
Original form	Original form	Original form	Computer-to-computer communication
Punched card	Punched card	None	None
Prepared by machine	Magnetic tape	None	None
Prepared by machine	Magnetic tape	Mass-storage device	Mass-storage Device
Manually prepared	Computer print-out	Computer print-out	Reports issued when requested by manager through inquiry station
Manually prepared	Manually prepared	Computer print-out	Computer print-out

The survey results show that systems designers have not yet accepted COBOL to any great extent. Auditor respondents complained about the inefficiency of the translator in developing a program which can be used in production runs. The COBOL translator is particularly inefficient on the smaller computers, making for implementation problems and lost time.

Indeed, by and large systems designers seem not yet to have mastered the "art" of installing computer systems in an efficient manner. The implementation phase of computer installation takes an unreasonable amount of time; this circumstance has exacerbated top management's dissatisfaction with computers. Routines supplied by equipment manufacturers have not always proven satisfactory, hence designers have had to develop service programs on an individual basis—an extremely costly procedure. All in all, the cost of installing a computer complex has tended to exceed primary estimates, mainly because of complications with available software. Increased standardization of service routines and general improvement in implementing computer systems are clearly in order if there is to be significant progress in developing integrated EDP systems.

The related problem of information retrieval has also interposed significant obstacles to installing business-oriented computer systems. Integrated data-processing systems require a large mass-storage file from which information may be retrieved rapidly and at a reasonable cost. Appropriate technology for this seems to be developing in the IBM system/360. NCR's CRAM (discussed in chapter iii) is also a contribution in this area. Considerable research is being done in the area of information retrieval and it seems clear that significant developments will be of major importance for integrated data processing.

DEVELOPMENTS IN AUDITING THEORY AND PRACTICE

Table 4 shows that the sequential development of integrated data-processing systems involves the gradual abandonment of the audit trail. All in-line accounting systems rely on some variant of mass-storage. The basic difference between batch-controlled systems and mass-storage (in-line) systems was discussed earlier: the updating of a record in the in-line mass-storage file supplants the balance previously stored in that memory location. The solutions proposed to maintain an audit trail in this situation are basically unsatisfactory.

If integrated data-processing systems become more sophisticated, internally generated source documents that the auditor relies on will also tend to disappear. The auditor will then be faced with having lost both the audit trail and the internally generated source document, two of the main cornerstones upon which audit programs have been built. And the advent of on-line, real-time computer systems will remove the final prop on which the auditor has relied historically. Documents traditionally used for inter-firm communication will no longer be needed in the business data-processing system.

Faced with these possible developments, the profession which only sits and waits surely serves the business community, and itself, very badly indeed. The urgency of adopting a forward-looking approach to the problems of auditing business-oriented computers cannot be overstated. Not only must the auditor be able to assure his client that financial statements fairly represent the financial condition as of a given date, he must be able also to isolate areas in the system where changes would be advantageous. The auditor already calls his client's attention to weaknesses in traditional business systems and offers advice about correcting these weaknesses—valuable functions indeed. It is essential that the auditor preserve and expand this function in dealing with

EDP systems. Patently, he must, then, have basic knowledge of the system and at least conceptual familiarity with its technology.

That there has been a lack of communication between the systems designers employed by the equipment manufacturers and the public accounting firm engaged by the client has hardly made various of the problems discussed in this study less oppressive. Neither should dominate the other—or needs to. But close coöperation is clearly desirable on matters in which both designers and auditors have a crucial interest. There must, for example, be mutual understanding of what is meant by internal control. There must be agreement on features of the system's data linkage. These and other joint decisions are essential to the design of a system which satisfies both the economic consideration of the client and the functional requirements essential to the verification of the financial statements.

IMPLICATIONS FOR THE FUTURE

With technology changing as rapidly as it is in EDP business information system development, there is an obvious need for continuous research, and even for some "daydreaming." The development of the computer audit programs themselves is merely the first phase of dealing with the problems of auditing business-oriented computer systems. Models must be subjected to repeated detailed tests in order to establish their applicability to various situations. This testing does not aim at changing the basic principles of the models, but it will continually lead to changes in some of the details—and sometimes to development of an essentially new model. Not only must the models be tested regarding their sensitivity to various areas that concern the auditor; they should also be checked against the conclusions of practicing accountants.

The concept of a business information system as it was outlined in chapter ii must also be subjected to a great deal of study by the accounting profession. The suggested approach does not start with specific segments of the firm; it starts with the over-all structure. But the accountant must be concerned with the details of decision data pertinent to marketing, production, and finance if he is to incorporate their requirements into the business information system. The interaction of over-all firm objectives with these functional areas requires a great deal of study and work, tapping the knowledge, the requirements, and the dissatisfactions of people concerned with decisions in the several areas.

Most systems are designed *ad hoc;* if we are to avoid the pitfalls of this approach, initial research should be at the theoretical level, leaving the testing of the concepts to supplementary research. But the investigator must also keep sound perspective, testing theoretical conclusions against the actual operation of systems. Case studies should prove to be useful in this reality checking.

The computer audit programs presented in chapter vi go beyond the current thinking of most of the profession. They add a decision-making function to the preprocessing of data that is necessary in any normal test-of-transactions audit program. This addition, in essence, replaces the decision-making function of the junior staff auditor. Theoretically, it is possible to extend the function of the computer audit program even beyond this level. When the computerized audit program has generated an evaluation of the business information system of the firm and conclusions about its relative strengths and weaknesses, auditing procedures might advance one step farther. In all auditing, after examining the system of internal control, the auditor develops the program for the remainder of the examination on the basis of his findings in that earlier stage. This step could be computerized in much the same way as was the test-of-transactions program for payroll and order processing. The computer would determine how much more sampling of the system of internal control should be done; it would also indicate the extent to which other audit procedures and techniques should be strengthened or curtailed. Eventually, the audit program—which is itself an information system—should be as fully integrated as the business information system it reviews. Nothing less will afford appropriate and adequate auditing of EDP business data.

APPENDIX A

Survey Questionnaire and Summary of Responses

INSTRUCTIONS FOR COMPLETING QUESTIONNAIRE

This questionnaire is designed to be completed in a minimum amount of time and, accordingly, is divided into two parts. Part A deals with auditing procedures and should be completed by an audit staff partner. Part B deals with electronic data processing systems and procedures and may be completed by the manager of the management services department or by the audit staff partner who completed Part A. If you feel that you are unable to answer a question for any reason, leave it blank and note the reason in the space provided in Question 40 on the last page of the questionnaire. The questionnaire refers only to the clients for which your office has primary responsibility rather than to the clients of the entire firm.

The results of the survey will be made available to the accounting profession. If you are particularly interested please enclose a stamped, addressed envelope with the completed questionnaire for a summary of the results when they become available. The questionnaires are numbered for purposes of statistical control, but in the ultimate report the information will be held in strictest confidence. The findings will in no way reveal the identity of those who participate in the survey.

A stamped, addressed envelope is enclosed for your convenience in returning the completed questionnaire. Thank you very much for your cooperation.

PART A

GENERAL QUESTIONS RELATING TO AUDITING PROCEDURES

1. Is your firm a:

                                                          (Check one)

   National firm of more than 20 offices   ☐ (25)

   National firm of from 5 to 20 offices   ☐ (0)

   Regional or national firm of from 2 to 5 offices   ☐ (0)

   Local firm   ☐ (0)

   Individual practitioner   ☐ (0)

2. How many employees including partners do you have on the
   audit staff of your office?   __(3273)__
                                   (Write in)

3. Approximately how many audit reports does your <u>office</u>
   issue on an annual basis?   __(14046)__
                                   (Write in)

4. Approximately how many of these clients with an annual
   sales volume of $20,000,000 or greater (or clients of
   comparable size in other industries) are:

Manufacturing____ (549)	Finance, Insurance or Real Estate ____ (234)	Services(Hotels or Professional) ____(63)
Wholesaling ____ (91)	Transportation (89)____	Government or Gov't Enterprise ____(17)
Retailing ____ (79)	Communication or Public Utilities ____ (66)	Miscellaneous ____(85)

5. Approximately what percentage of these clients:

                                        (Check a % figure for each line)

   Have a punched-card installation only
                                        52.0%
   ├┼┼┼┼┼▼┼┼┼┼┤
   0%1 2 3 4 50% 6 7 8 9 100%

   Have their own tape-oriented
     computer installation   22.3%
   ├┼┼▼┼┼┼┼┼┼┼┤
   0%1 2 3 4 50% 6 7 8 9 100%

   Rent time on other computers   12.4%
   ├┼▼┼┼┼┼┼┼┼┼┤
   0%1 2 3 4 50% 6 7 8 9 100%

6. What changes have you made in your audit programs for clients who
   have a punched-card installation only?

                                                          (Check one)
   Usually make no changes   ☐ (0)

   Sometimes make minor changes. That is, it can
   be adequately handled by the senior in charge
   of the engagement subject to appropriate review   ☐ (23)

   Usually make significant changes. That is, the
   audit procedures must be completely reviewed
   and revised   ☐ (6)

   Have no such clients   ☐ (0)

-2-

7. Approximately what percentage of your clients who have a tape-oriented computer process the following functions on this equipment?

Function	(Check a % figure for each line)

Payroll
82.4%
0% 1 2 3 4 50% 6 7 8 9 100%

Billing and accounts receivable
78.2%
0% 1 2 3 4 50% 6 7 8 9 100%

Accounts payable
35.2%
0% 1 2 3 4 50% 6 7 8 9 100%

Inventory control
47.5%
0% 1 2 3 4 50% 6 7 8 9 100%

Production control
19.4%
0% 1 2 3 4 50% 6 7 8 9 100%

Scientific research
14.4%
0% 1 2 3 4 50% 6 7 8 9 100%

Other (Please specify)_____
4.0%
0% 1 2 3 4 50% 6 7 8 9 100%

8. Approximately how many of your clients' tape-oriented computer installations for processing accounting information can be classified as:

(Enter number on each line)

A batch-control system using magnetic tapes or punched cards as the typical storage medium for master records ___(172)___

A random-access (in-line) accounting system using some type of disc file storage for updated master files ___(35)___

A combination of a batch-control system and an in-line accounting system ___(44)___

An integrated data-processing system utilizing the concept of point-of-sale recording with a minimum of manual data manipulation between the transaction and the relevant operating reports ___(20)___

Other (Please specify)_____ ___(13)___

TOTAL COMPUTER INSTALLATIONS   284

9. Referring to those clients who have tape-oriented computer, in approximately what percentage[*] of the cases does the data processing manager report to:

Title	Number of Cases
President	(11)
Executive Vice President	(47)
Vice President, Finance	(53)
Controller	(152)
Assistant Controller	(11)
Other (Please specify) _____	(10)
TOTAL	284

[*] Answers received were in percentages but were converted to nearest whole numbers for purposes of this study.

10. What new control techniques have been implemented which
    are peculiar to the use of electronic equipment (for
    example, console logs or tape libraries)? Please list
    the more important techniques

    1. Use of console logs as a control device _____ (10)

    2. Use of controlled tape libraries _____ (8)

    3. Implementation of formal program change procedure _____ (6)

    4. Internal and external tape label checks _____ (4)

    5. Use of hash control totals _____ (4)

    6. Emphasis on internal control of data-processing division (3)

    7. Use of simulated data tests _____ (3)

    8. Thorough documentation of computer operating techniques (2)

    9. Tape record counts _____ (1)

    10. Use of grandfather-father back-up tapes _____ (1)

    11. None _____ (2)

11. Approximately how many members of your audit staff
    have at least the following qualifications?

                                          (Enter a number
                                          on each line)

    Basic understanding of the internal logic of the
    computer, including ability to write in the basic
    programming languages   (192)

    General understanding of the input-output equip-
    ment and some knowledge of the internal controls
    which are built into the computer   (565)

    General understanding of how computers function
    and an ability to read and interpret "flow
    charts" and "block diagrams" of computer systems   (640)

    Have none of the above   (900)

12. What degree of proficiency with the computer do
    you feel is desirable for staff accountants
    who audit EDP installations?

                                            (Check one)

    Basic understanding of the internal logic of
    the computer, including ability to write in
    the basic programming languages   ☐ (0)

    General understanding of the input-output
    equipment and some knowledge of the internal
    controls which are built into the computer   ☐ (20)

    General understanding of how computers function
    and an ability to read and interpret "flow
    charts" and "block diagrams" of computer systems   ☐ (6)

    None of the above   ☐ (0)

-4-

13. In your formal staff training programs how do you handle the role of computers in business systems?

(Check as many as apply)

Each subject matter area in the staff training program is considered from the standpoint of computer-oriented systems as well as traditional data processing systems ☐ (9)

It is introduced as a separate topic without specific reference to individual sections of the audit program ☐ (12)

Formal study is restricted to supervisory audit and management services personnel ☐ (11)

This phase of staff training is handled by sending selected audit staff personnel to computer manufacturers or universities for technical training ☐ (10)

This subject is not taught as a formal part of the staff training program ☐ (0)

14. How should electronic data processing (EDP) training be provided for the audit staff?

Staff training meetings	(14)
On-the-job training for specific assignments	(8)
Use of computer manufacturer's service courses	(7)
Part of advanced staff training for seniors	(2)
Use of case studies	(2)
Informal study with management services personnel	(1)
Use of correspondence courses	(1)

15. Do you feel that it is desirable during the design and installation phases of an EDP system to have the audit staff partner or manager in charge of the client make periodic visits to review the progress of the installation?

(Check one)

Yes ☐ (20)

Seldom necessary since an adequate review can be made during the preliminary work for the annual examination ☐ (2)

Our policy is to discourage such visits and to limit the supervision to management services personnel ☐ (3)

Other (Please specify)_____

_____ ☐ (0)

This question is not applicable to our office ☐ (0)

16. What changes have you made in your audit programs
for clients who have their own tape-oriented
computer installations?

(Check one)

Usually make no changes   ☐ (0)

Sometimes make minor changes. That is, it can
be adequately handled by the senior in charge
of the engagement subject to appropriate review   ☐ (9)

Usually make significant changes. That is, the
audit procedures must be completely reviewed and
revised   ☐ (14)

Have no such clients   ☐ (2)

17. How often are the following techniques used in auditing
    batch controlled (off-line) EDP installations?

(Check one box on each line)

	Always	Usually	Seldom	Never
Use of conventional "audit trail" records	☐ (14)	☐ (5)	☐ (5)	☐ (0)
Use of controlled data (test deck) to review client's computer program	☐ (1)	☐ (10)	☐ (6)	☐ (5)
Maintenance of a controlled copy of client's program tape to periodically test client's program tape (or output)	☐ (0)	☐ (1)	☐ (8)	☐ (14)
Use of an independent audit program written in a problem-oriented language which is prepared by the public accounting firm for use in testing the output of the client's computer program	☐ (0)	☐ (2)	☐ (10)	☐ (8)
Other (Please specify)_____ _____	☐ (3)	☐ (0)	☐ (0)	☐ (0)

Have had no experience in auditing off-line EDP installations   ☐ (2)

-6-

18. How often are the following techniques used in auditing
    mass-storage (in-line) EDP installations?

    (Check one box on each line)

	Always	Usually	Seldom	Never
Use of conventional "audit trail" records	☐(8)	☐ (8)	☐ (0)	☐ (0)
Use of controlled data (test deck) to review client's computer program	☐(5)	☐ (2)	☐ (6)	☐ (3)
Maintenance of a controlled copy of client's program tape to periodically test client's program tape (or output)	☐ (1)	☐ (0)	☐ (8)	☐ (7)
Use of an independent audit program written in a problem-oriented language which is prepared by the public accounting form for use in testing the output of the client's computer program	☐ (0)	☐(2)	☐ (7)	☐ (8)
Other (please specify)_____	☐ (1)	☐(0)	☐ (0)	☐ (1)

    Have had no experience in auditing in-line EDP installations ☐ (9)

19. How useful are the reports of internal auditors in
    reviewing the internal controls of an EDP installation?

    (Check one)

    Extremely useful   ☐ (4)

    Moderately useful   ☐ (7)

    Seldom useful   ☐ (6)

    This question is not applicable   ☐ (7)

    If your answer is either moderately useful or seldom
    useful, what are the major deficiencies in the reports
    of internal auditors?

    Lack of EDP knowledge on the part of internal auditors   (6)

    Seldom able to do more than make random tests   (1)

    Lack of coordination between internal and external auditors (1)

20. How often do you retain the following information in the
   permanent file section of the audit work papers?

(Check one box for each line)

	Always	Usually	Seldom	Never
EDP system "flow charts"	☐ (11)	☐ (3)	☐ (5)	☐ (4)
EDP system "block diagrams"	☐ (9)	☐ (2)	☐ (5)	☐ (6)
Copies of computer programs	☐ (5)	☐ (1)	☐ (4)	☐ (12)
Descriptions of computer hardware	☐ (6)	☐ (7)	☐ (1)	☐ (8)
Samples of EDP output	☐ (4)	☐ (9)	☐ (2)	☐ (8)
Have no such clients	☐ (2)			

21. What, in your opinion, will be the major changes, if any,
   to be made in audit procedures so far as internal control
   and data processing are concerned as a result of the
   increase use of electronic computers in processing data
   for business information systems?

Greater emphasis on internal and external data control	(6)
Greater emphasis on procedure reviews and program testing	(4)
Use of test decks to review computer audit programs	(5)
Surprise visits to observe computer operations	(3)
More effective utilization of internal auditors	(2)
Need for increased knowledge on part of auditors	(1)
Use of computer programs written by the auditor	(1)
Development of computer audit program in cooperation with client	(1)
Use of computer as a tool to do detail audit work	(1)

22. What is your position with the firm?

Partner (21)
Manager (4)

If you have any comments to make on Part A of the questionnaire,
please make them here:

(1) The questionnaire is too condensed. Specific case studies would be
a better approach.

(2) Some of questions require only a general answer. Questions should
be more specific.

THIS COMPLETES PART A OF THE QUESTIONNAIRE, PART B STARTS ON NEXT PAGE

-8-

PART B

QUESTIONS RELATING TO EDP SYSTEMS AND PROCEDURES

23. How many employees including partners do you have in
    the management services department of your office?   (447)
                                                          ‾‾‾‾‾‾‾‾‾‾‾
                                                          (Write in)

    If none, check one of the following:

    Have a working relationship with management services
    departments in offices of our firm in other cities   ☐ (0)

    Handle management services assignments by using
    regular members of the audit staff   ☐ (0)

    Other (Please specify) _____   ☐ (0)
    _____

24. How many "specialists" on EDP do you
    have in your office?   (169)
                          ‾‾‾‾‾‾‾‾‾‾‾
                          (Write in)

    If none, check one of the following:

    Have a working relationship with management services
    departments in offices of our firm in other cities   ☐ (0)

    Hire outside consultants or rely on the
    computer manufacturers for technical advice   ☐ (0)

    Have no clients with EDP systems   ☐ (0)

25. Does the management services department:
                                                          (Check one)
    Train its own EDP "specialists" from among personnel
    who already have accounting training   ☐ (6)

    Prefer to train its own "specialists" but also hire
    "specialists" who are not necessarily trained   ☐ (9)
    accountants

    Primarily hire trained EDP "specialists"   ☐ (9)

    We do not have any EDP "specialists"   ☐ (0)

26. How many of your EDP "specialists" can write programs in:
                                        (Enter number on each line)

            COBOL   _____(47)_____

            FORTRAN   _____(38)_____

            ALGOL   _____(29)_____

            Other (Please specify)
            Various symbolic languages ____(159)____

27. When your office assists a client in installing a tape-
oriented computer, to what extent do the following
personnel participate?

(Check one box on each line)

	Great Extent	Moderate Extent	Limited Extent	Don't Participate
Audit partner in charge of the client	☐ (1)	☐ (7)	☐ (15)	☐ (1)
Audit manager assigned to the client	☐ (6)	☐ (4)	☐ (13)	☐ (1)
Audit staff accountants	☐ (0)	☐ (2)	☐ (12)	☐ (10)
Other (Please specify) _____	☐	☐	☐	☐
Not applicable		☐ (1)		

28. Approximately how many EDP "feasibility" studies has your
office participated in since January 1, 1960? __(332)__
(Write in)

If one or more, how many of these studies
were implemented?

__(229)__
(Write in)

29. Approximately how many assignments has your office had
since January 1, 1960 which involved the possible abandonment of an existing tape-oriented computer?

__(31)__
(Write in)

If one or more, how many of these installations were
actually abandoned?   __(8)__
(Write in)

30. Of the EDP "feasibility" studies which your office has
participated   approximately what percentage*of them involved:

	Number
Purchase of a substantially identical additional computer	(3)
Replacement of an existing computer with a new type of computer designed by the same manufacturer	(40)
Replacement of an existing computer with that of a different manufacturer	(22)
Conversion from a punched-card installation	(209)
Conversion from a manual system	(50)
Other (Please specify) _____	(8)

* Answers received were in percentages but were converted to
nearest whole numbers for purposes of this study.

-10-

31. In reviewing tape-oriented computer installations for possible
    alterations or improvements, what, in your opinion, have been
    the major weaknesses in existing techniques and procedures?

Inefficient system design	(15)	Poor integration with accounting system	(1)
Poor documentation of EDP system	(8)	Poor "software"	(1)
Controls are too centralized	(2)	Poor use of computer output	(1)
Lack of input-output controls	(2)	Poor scheduling	(1)
No economic justification	(2)	Need for random-access equipment	(1)

32. How many employee defalcations have been discovered among
    your clients since January 1, 1960, which are related to
    the use of electronic data processing equipment? ___(6)___
                                                        (Write in)

    If one or more, describe very briefly the methods by
    which the frauds were perpetrated:

Card substitution or alteration	(4)
Night work when computer unattended	(1)
Collusion between key-punch and console operators	(1)

33. In the literature, there has been considerable discussion
    of the possibility of the unauthorized intervention of the
    console operator. How does your firm handle this problem?

Use and control of console log	(8)
Manual intervention eliminated by adoption of standard operating procedures	(8)
Separation of duties	(5)
Controls maintained by internal auditors	(3)
Control of program changes	(1)
Planned and operating time comparisons	(1)
Programmed print-out of key-entered data	(1)
Surprise tests by independent auditors	(1)

34. In designing EDP techniques and procedures, how much emphasis
    do you place on:

(Check one box on each line)

	Great Emphasis	Moderate Emphasis	Little Emphasis	None
Separating the duties of the programmers from those of the operators	☐ (16)	☐ (5)	☐ (1)	☐ (0)
Establishing an independent center for preparing data for input to the computer	☐ (10)	☐ (11)	☐ (1)	☐ (1)
Separating the data processing center from the Accounting department	☐ (7)	☐ (7)	☐ (7)	☐ (3)
Using internal auditors to strengthen internal controls on the data processing center	☐ (9)	☐ (3)	☐ (12)	☐ (0)
Use of post-audit techniques to control the operation of the data processing center	☐ (5)	☐ (12)	☐ (4)	☐ (1)
Other (Please specify)_____ Intensive use of internal and external total controls	☐ (1)	☐ (1)	☐ (0)	☐ (0)
Documentation of procedures	(1)	(1)	(0)	(0)

This question is not applicable to our office ☐ (2)

35. How often do the following potential problems occur in the
implementation of client's EDP systems?

(Check one box on each line)

	Always	Usually	(Sometimes)*	Seldom	Never
Availability of qualified company personnel	☐ (4)	☐ (16)		☐ (3)	☐ (0)
Underestimation of equipment time requirements	☐ (0)	☐ (10)		☐ (11)	☐ (1)
Reliability of central processor	☐ (0)	☐ (1)		☐ (12)	☐ (7)
Reliability of input-output devices	☐ (0)	☐ (9)	(2)	☐ (9)	☐ (2)
Acceptance by managerial and supervisory personnel	☐ (2)	☐ (8)	(1)	☐ (12)	☐ (0)
Availability of "software"	☐ (2)	☐ (8)	(2)	☐ (9)	☐ (1)
Other (Please specify)	☐	☐		☐	☐
Inadequate testing and documentation	(0)	(2)		(0)	(0)
Oversimplification by salesmen	(1)	(0)		(0)	(0)
Analysis of time and costs	(1)	(1)		(0)	(0)

This question is not applicable to our office   ☐

* Inserted by respondents

36. In your opinion, what is the future of COBOL (Common
Business Oriented Language)?

Looks good at present	(4)
It is several years off	(3)
Needs to be modified	(3)
It will be replaced	(3)
It is limited	(3)
Common language impractical	(2)
It is too complex	(1)
Will standardize programming	(1)
Not for production runs	(1)
Useful as a bridge between systems	(1)

-12-

37. If you were to prepare a recommendation for the manufacturers of computer hardware, what importance would you place on research in each of the following areas?

(Check one box on each line)

	Primary Importance	Great Importance	Little Importance
Further developments in mass-storage memory devices	☐ (8)	☐ (12)	☐ (5)
Universal adoption of a problem-oriented language	☐ (8)	☐ (11)	☐ (6)
Additional emphasis on data input conversion devices such as optical scanners	☐ (11)	☐ (14)	☐ (1)
Development of higher speed peripheral equipment	☐ (6)	☐ (12)	☐ (7)
Development of lower cost computer hardware	☐ (9)	☐ (9)	☐ (5)
Development of techniques and methods which will substantially reduce installation costs	☐ (10)	☐ (11)	☐ (4)
Other (Please specify) _____ Change in rentals during early months	☐ (1)	☐ (0)	☐ (0)
Solution of programming problems by other means than programming	(1)	(0)	(0)

38. In your opinion, what are the major problems involved in the development of integrated data processing systems?

Competency of personnel	(10)
Definition of the system	(8)
Costs of data transmission	(6)
Management non-acceptance	(5)
Time required for design and installation	(3)
Control problems with input data	(3)
Problem of balancing system	(2)
Programming difficulties with systems	(2)
Lack of flexibility of EDP system	(1)

39. What is your position with the firm?

Partner	(17)
Principal	(1)
Manager of Data Processing	(7)

40. It is inevitable in a questionnaire of this type that answers might be restricted by limitations on the choices imposed by the design of the questionnaire. In some cases, it is conceivable that the question can not be answered at all. Therefore, it will be appreciated if any such explanatory comments can be indicated in the spaces provided below:

Question No.	Comments
	No comments noted

Thank you for your cooperation. We would be most appreciative of any further comments you wish to make. Please add them here. Use the reverse side of the page if necessary.

Computer Audit Program for Test of a Factory Payroll

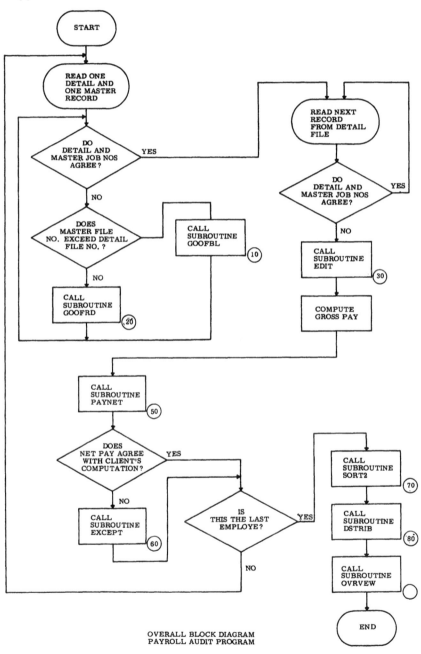

OVERALL BLOCK DIAGRAM
PAYROLL AUDIT PROGRAM

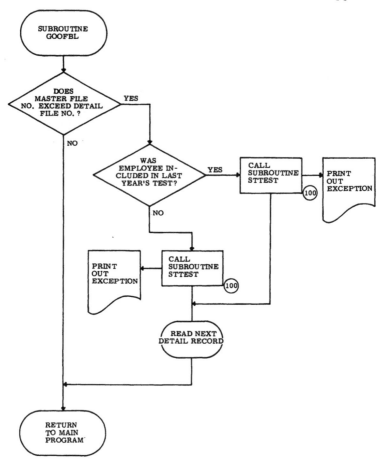

SUBROUTINE GOOFBL - DETAIL (10)

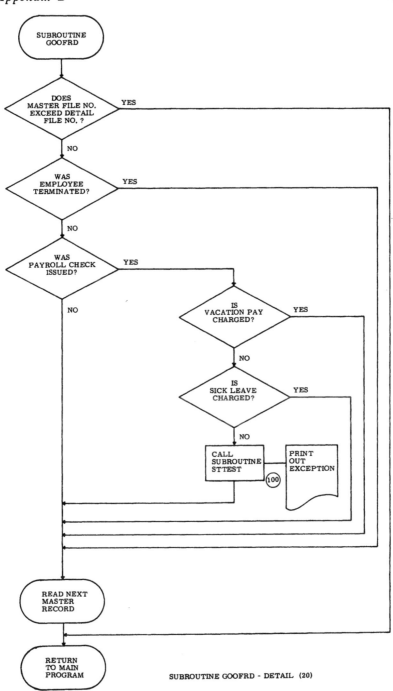

SUBROUTINE GOOFRD - DETAIL (20)

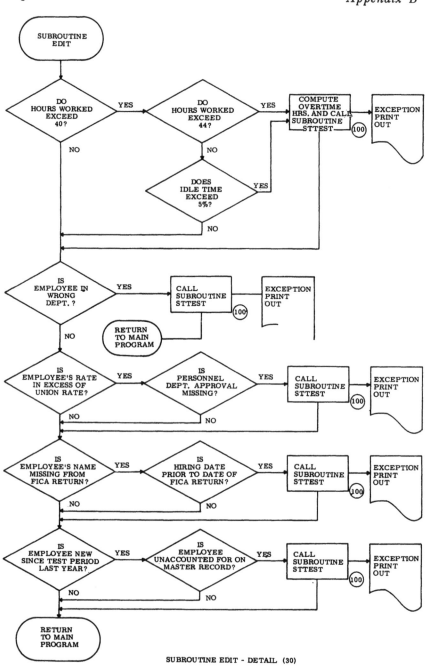

SUBROUTINE EDIT - DETAIL (30)

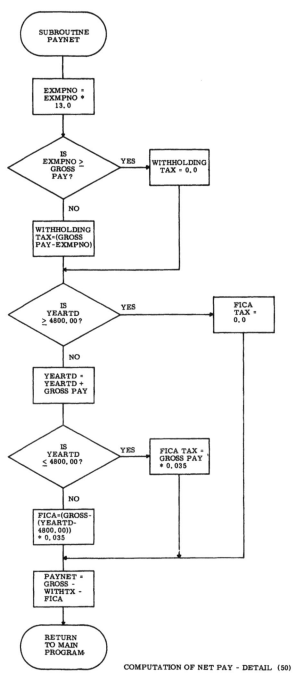

COMPUTATION OF NET PAY - DETAIL (50)

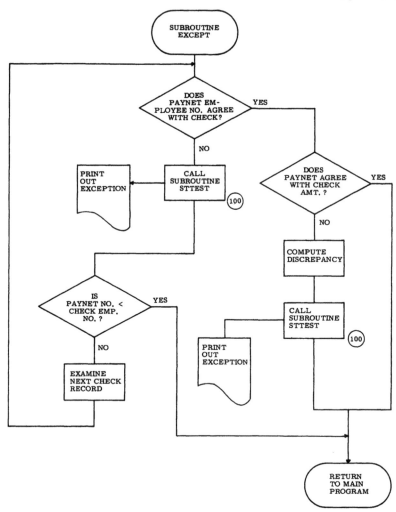

SUBROUTINE EXCEPT - DETAIL (60)

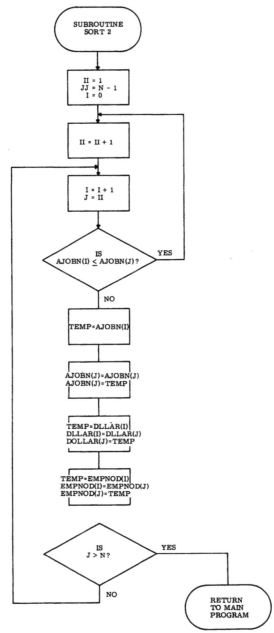

SUBROUTINE SORT 2 - DETAIL (70)

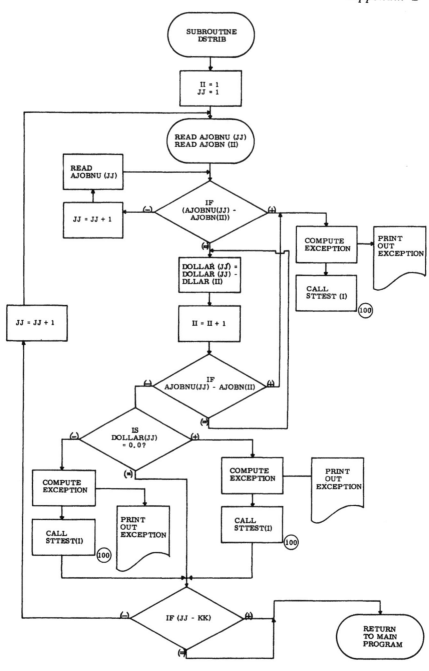

SUBROUTINE DSTRIB - DETAIL (80)

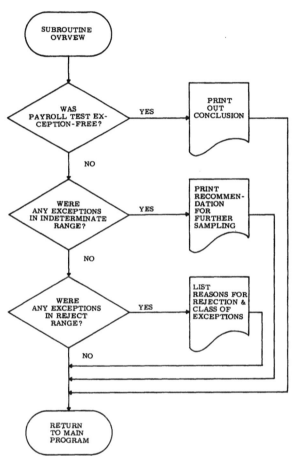

SUBROUTINE OVRVEW - DETAIL (90)

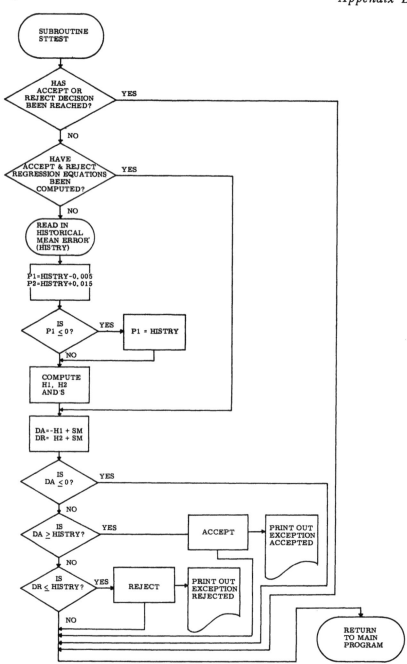

SUBROUTINE
STTEST

HAS
ACCEPT OR
REJECT DECISION
BEEN REACHED? — YES

NO

HAVE
ACCEPT & REJECT
REGRESSION EQUATIONS
BEEN
COMPUTED? — YES

NO

READ IN
HISTORICAL
MEAN ERROR'
(HISTRY)

P1=HISTRY-0.005
P2=HISTRY+0.015

IS
P1 ≤ 0? — YES — P1 = HISTRY

NO

COMPUTE
H1, H2
AND 'S

DA=-H1 + SM
DR= H2 + SM

IS
DA ≤ 0? — YES

NO

IS
DA ≥ HISTRY? — YES — ACCEPT — PRINT OUT
EXCEPTION
ACCEPTED

NO

IS
DR ≤ HISTRY? — YES — REJECT — PRINT OUT
EXCEPTION
REJECTED

NO

RETURN
TO MAIN
PROGRAM

Sequential sampling equations adapted from: R. M. and H. Justin Davidson, Statistical
Sampling for Accounting Information (Englewood Cliffs, N. J., 1962, Prentice-Hall,
Inc.), pp. 163-165.

SUBROUTINE STTEST - DETAIL (100)

```
                       MAIN PAYROLL PROGRAM
       COMMON M,N,L,K,MM,LL,KK,EMPNO1,CLASS1,HOURP1,HIRED1,YEART1,EXMPN1,
      1 TERMD1,EMPNOD,AJOBN,HOURW,SHIFT,EMPNO2,EXMPN2,CLASS2,HOURP2,HIRED
      22,YEART2,TERMD2,EMPNO3,CLASS3,HOURP3,HIRED3,YEART3,TERMD3,EXMPN3,
      3EMPNO,FICADT,EMPNBR,GRPAY,FWT,SSTAX,TAKHOM,EMPNO4,AJOBNU,CHARGE,
      4AMOUNT,ACLASS,DOLLAR,HISTRY,SAMPNO,DATA,INDEX,TIMIDL,DLLAR,GROSS,
      5PYNET,DIST,WTHTAX,FICA,PERCNT,TOT,REJECT,FINAL
       DIMENSION EMPNO1(300),EXMPN1(300),CLASS1(300),HOURP1(300),HIRED1(3
      100),YEART1(300),TERMD1(300),EMPNOD(300),AJOBN(300),HOURW(300),SHIF
      2T(300),EMPNO2(300),EXMPN2(300),CLASS2(300),HOURP2(300),HIRED2(300)
      3,YEART2(300),TERMD2(300),EMPNO3(300),EXMPN3(300),CLASS3(300),HOURP
      43(300),HIRED3(300),YEART3(300),TERMD3(300),EMPNO(300),FICADT(300),
      5EMPNBR(300),GRPAY(300),FWT(300),SSTAX(300),TAKHOM(300),EMPNO4(300)
      6,AJOBNU(300),CHARGE(300),AMOUNT(300),ACLASS(300),DOLLAR(300),HISTR
      7Y(20),DATA(20),INDEX(20),P1(20),P2(20),H1(20),H2(20),S(20),DA(20),
      8DR(20),FINAL(20),DLLAR(300),TIMIDL(300),GROSS(300),PYNET(300),DIST
      9(300),WTHTAX(300),FICA(300),TOT(300),REJECT(20)
       READ 2,M,N,L,K,MM,LL,KK
     2 FORMAT(7I4)
C      M IS NUMBER OF MASTER RECORDS IN LAST YEARS PAYROLL TEST.
C      NIS NUMBER OF DETAIL RECORDS IN CURRENT PERIOD TEST.
     4 READ 6,(EMPNO1(J),EXMPN1(J),CLASS1(J),HOURP1(J),HIRED1(J),YEART1(J
      1),TERMD1(J),J=1,M)
       READ 8,(EMPNOD(I),AJOBN(I),HOURW(I),SHIFT(I),I=1,N)
C      L IS NUMBER OF MASTER RECORDS IN BEGINNING OF TEST PERIOD FILE.
C      K IS NUMBER OF MASTER RECORDS IN END OF TEST PERIOD FILE.
       READ 6,(EMPNO2(J),EXMPN2(J),CLASS2(J),HOURP2(J),HIRED2(J),YEART2(J
      1),TERMD2(J),J=1,L)
       READ 6,(EMPNO3(J),EXMPN3(J),CLASS3(J),HOURP3(J),HIRED3(J),YEART3(J
      1),TERMD3(J),J=1,K)
       READ 10, (EMPNO(J),FICADT(J),J=1,MM)
C      MM IS NUMBER OF EMPLOYES ON SOCIAL SECURITY QUARTERLY TAX REPORT
       READ 12,(EMPNBR(J),GRPAY(J),FWT(J),SSTAX(J),TAKHOM(J),J=1,LL)
C      LL IS NUMBER OF PAYROLL CHECKS ISSUED FOR TEST PERIOD.
       READ 14,(EMPNO4(J),AJOBNU(J),CHARGE(J),AMOUNT(J),ACLASS(J),DOLLAR(
      1J),J=1,KK)
C      KK IS NUMBER OF LABOR DISTRIBUTION RECORDS.
       READ 116,(HISTRY(I),I=1,15)
   116 FORMAT(F4.3)
    14 FORMAT (3F4.0,F4.2,F4.0,F7.2)
    12 FORMAT(F4.0,F6.2,2F5.2,F6.2)
    10 FORMAT (F4.0,F6.0)
     8 FORMAT (2F4.0,F5.3,F3.2)
     6 FORMAT (F4.0,2F2.0,F5.3,F6.0,F7.2,F6.0)
       NN=0
       READ 114,A,B,C,D
   114 FORMAT(4F10.3)
C      A=NUMBER OF EMPLOYES IN THE ACTIVE PAYROLL FILE PER PERSONNEL DEPT.
C      B=HASH TOTAL OF EMPLOYE NUMBERS ACCORDING TO PERSONNEL DEPT.
C      C=HASH TOTAL OF EMPLOYE PAY RATES ACCORDING TO PERSONNEL DEPT.
C      D=HASH TOTAL OF EXEMPTION NUMBERS ACCORDING TO PERSONNEL DEPT.
C      THIS WILL BE THE LAST DATA CARD.
       PUNCH 22,K
    22 FORMAT(50H1DETAIL OF EXCEPTIONS NOTED DURING TEST PERIOD FOR,I3,9H
      1 EMPLOYES//)
C      THE OUTPUT TAPE IS LABELED
       CALL HASH(A,B,C,D)
     5 DO 30 J=1,L
       SAMPNO=J
C      NN IS THE COUNTER FOR INDIVIDUAL TIME CARDS
```

```
      NN=NN+1
  111 IF(EMPNOD(NN)-EMPNO2(J))1,3,100
    1 CALL GOOFBL(J,NN)
      GO TO 111
    3 SUM=0.0
      DLLAR(NN)=HOURP2(J)*HOURW(NN)
    7 SUM=SUM+HOURW(NN)
      IF(AJOBN(NN)-2000.)71,78,71
   78 TIMIDL(J)=TIMIDL(J)+HOURW(NN)
   71 NN=NN+1
      IF(NN-N)72,72,9
   72 IF(EMPNOD(NN)-EMPNO2(J))1,7,9
    9 NN=NN-1
      HOURW(J)=SUM
      CALL EDIT(J,NN)
      IF(HOURW(J)-40.0)11,11,13
   13 HOURW(J)=HOURW(J)+(HOURW(J)-40.0)/2.0
   11 HOURW(J)=HOURW(J)*SHIFT(NN)
      GROSS(J)=HOURW(J)*HOURP2(J)
      CALL PAYNET(J,NN)
      CALL EXCEPT(J,NN)
      IF(J-L)30,19,19
   19 PUNCH 24
   24 FORMAT(79HOREVIEW OF LABOR DISTRIBUTION PROCEDURE. IF NO COMMENT I
     1S MADE, NO ERRORS NOTED)
      CALL SORT2
      CALL DSTRIB
      PUNCH 110
      PUNCH 112
  110 FORMAT(64H1SUMMARY OF EXCEPTIONS NOTED DURING THE TEST OF INTERNAL
     1 CONTROL/44HEXCEPTION NUMBERS ARE IDENTIFIED AS FOLLOWS./45H 1.TIM
     2E CARD IS MISSING BUT EMPLOYE WAS PAID./51H 2.MASTER CARD IS MISSI
     3NG BUT EMPLOYE WAS NOT PAID./78H 3.MASTER CARD IS MISSING, EMPLOYE
     4 WAS NOT PAID AND HE WAS IN LAST YEARS TEST./80H 4.MASTER CARD IS
     5MISSING, EMPLOYE WAS PAID AND HE WAS IN TEST PERIOD LAST YEAR./49H
     6 5.EMPLOYE IS CLASSIFIED IN THE WRONG DEPARTMENT./81H 6.HASH TOTAL
     7 OF MASTER PERSONNEL FILE DOES NOT AGREE WITH PERSONNEL DEPT. COUN
     8T./57H 7.OVERTIME PAID BUT IDLE TIME IS IN EXCESS OF 5 PERCENT./22
     9H 8.EXCESSIVE PAY RATE./34H 9.EMPLOYE NOT ON F.I.C.A. RETURN.)
  112 FORMAT(48H 10.ERROR IN HIRING DATE ON MASTER PAYROLL FILE./37H 11.
     1TIME TICKET NOT CHARGED TO A JOB./29H 12.LABOR DISTRIBUTION ERROR.
     2/60H 13.EMPLOYE THAT WORKED DURING THE TEST PERIOD WAS NOT PAID./5
     36H 14.ERROR IN NET PAY CALCULATION OF MORE THAN 5 PERCENT./53H 15.
     4ERROR IN NET PAY CALCULATION LESS THAN 5 PERCENT.)
      CALL OVRVEW(J,NN)
      GO TO 30
  100 CALL GOOFRD(J,NN)
   30 CONTINUE
      CALL EXIT
      END

      SUBROUTINE HASH(A,B,C,D)
C     COMMON AND DIMENSION STATEMENTS DELETED
      BSUM=0.0
      CSUM=0.0
      DSUM=0.0
      SAMPNO=0.0
      DO 50 J=1,L
      BSUM=BSUM+EMPNO2(J)
      CSUM=CSUM+HOURP2(J)
```

```
      DSUM=DSUM+EXMPN2(J)
   50 CONTINUE
      AL=L
      IF(A-AL)10,21,10
   21 IF(B-BSUM)11,22,11
   22 IF(C-CSUM)12,23,12
   23 IF(D-DSUM)13,100,13
   10 ATOTAL=A-AL
      PUNCH 2,ATOTAL
    2 FORMAT(77H 6. MASTER PERSONNEL FILE RECORD COUNT DISAGREES WITH PE
     1RSONNEL DEPT.COUNT BY,F3.0)
      I=6
      SAMPNO=SAMPNO+1.
      DATA(I)=DATA(I)+1.
      CALL STTEST(I)
      GO TO 21
   11 BTOTAL=B-BSUM
      PUNCH 4,BTOTAL
    4 FORMAT(72H 6. HASH TOTAL OF EMPLOYE NUMBERS DISAGREES WITH PERSONN
     1EL DEPT.COUNT BY,F8.0)
      I=6
      SAMPNO=SAMPNO+1.
      DATA(I)=DATA(I)+1.
      CALL STTEST (I)
      GO TO 22
   12 CTOTAL=C-CSUM
      PUNCH 6,CTOTAL
    6 FORMAT(73H 6. EMPLOYE HOURLY RATE HASH TOTAL DISAGREES WITH PERSON
     1NEL DEPT.COUNT BY,F7.3)
      I=6
      SAMPNO=SAMPNO+1.
      DATA(I)=DATA(I)+1.
      CALL STTEST(I)
      GO TO 23
   13 DTOTAL=D-DSUM
      PUNCH 8,DTOTAL
    8 FORMAT(72H 6. EMPLOYE EXEMPTION HASH TOTAL DISAGREES WITH PERSONNE
     1L DEPT.COUNT BY ,F6.0)
      I=6
      SAMPNO=SAMPNO+1.
      DATA(I)=DATA(I)+1.
      CALL STTEST(I)
  100 RETURN
      END

      SUBROUTINE GOOFBL(J,NN)
C     COMMON AND DIMENSION STATEMENTS DELETED
      IF(EMPNOD(NN)-EMPNO2(J))20,50,50
   20 II=1
   21 IF(EMPNO1(II)-EMPNOD(NN))25,30,35
   25 II=II+1
      IF(II-M)22,22,35
C     35 INDICATES MASTER CARD WAS MISSING LAST YEAR.
   22 GO TO 21
   35 JJ=1
   36 IF(EMPNBR(JJ)-EMPNOD(NN))40,46,44
   40 JJ=JJ+1
      IF(JJ-LL)41,41,44
   41 GO TO 36
C     44 INDICATES THAT NO PAYROLL CHECK WAS ISSUED.
```

```
   44 PUNCH 31,EMPNOD(NN)
   31 FORMAT(74H 2. MASTER PERSONNEL RECORD IS MISSING BUT EMPLOYE WAS N
      10T PAID, CLOCK NO.,F6.0)
      I=2
      DATA(I)=DATA(I)+1.
      CALL STTEST(I)
      GO TO 50
   30 JJ=1
  136 IF(EMPNBR(JJ)-EMPNOD(NN))140,42,144
  140 JJ=JJ+1
      IF(JJ-LL)141,141,144
  141 GO TO 136
  144 PUNCH 131,EMPNOD(NN)
  131 FORMAT(71H 3. MASTER RECORD MISSING THIS YEAR BUT EMPLOYE WAS NOT
      1PAID, CLOCK NO.,F6.0)
      I=3
      DATA(I)=DATA(I)+1.
      CALL STTEST(I)
      GO TO 50
   46 I=4
      DATA(I)=DATA(I)+1.
      PUNCH 146,EMPNOD(NN),GRPAY(JJ)
  146 FORMAT(50H 4. MASTER PERSONNEL RECORD IS MISSING, CLOCK NO. ,F5.0,
      17H PAID $,F6.2)
      GO TO 50
   42 PUNCH 33,EMPNOD(NN),GRPAY(JJ)
   33 FORMAT(49H 4. MASTER RECORD MISSING THIS YEAR, EMPLOYE NO. ,F5.0,7
      1H PAID $,F7.2)
      I=4
      DATA(I)=DATA(I)+1.
      CALL STTEST(I)
   50 NN=NN+1
      RETURN
      END

      SUBROUTINE EDIT(J,NN)
C     COMMON AND DIMENSION STATEMENTS DELETED
      IF(HOURW(J)-40.0)10,10,20
   20 IF(HOURW(J)-44.0)11,11,21
   11 PERCNT=TIMIDL(J)/HOURW(J)
   21 IF(PERCNT-0.05)10,10,211
  211 I=7
      DATA(I)=DATA(I)+1.
      PUNCH 40,EMPNO2(J)
   40 FORMAT(74H 7. OVERTIME PAID BUT IDLE TIME IN EXCESS OF 5 PERCENT,
      1EMPLOYE CLOCK NO. ,F5.0)
   10 IF(EMPNOD(NN)-5000.)12,13,13
   12 IF(EMPNOD(NN)-4001.)13,14,14
   13 I=5
      DATA(I)=DATA(I)+1.
      PUNCH 113,EMPNOD(NN)
  113 FORMAT(43H 5. EMPLOYE IS IN WRONG DEPT., CLOCK NUMBER,F5.0)
      CALL STTEST(I)
   14 IF(HOURP2(J)-3.50)16,16,17
   17 I=8
      DATA(I)=DATA(I)+1.
      PUNCH 117,HOURP2(J),EMPNO2(J)
  117 FORMAT(54H 8. HOURLY PAY RATE IS IN EXCESS OF UNION SCALE RATE $,F
      15.2,11H CLOCK NO. ,F5.0)
      CALL STTEST(I)
```

```
   16 JJ=1
  116 IF(EMPNO(JJ)-EMPNO2(J))18,22,19
   18 JJ=JJ+1
      GO TO 116
   19 IF(FICADT(JJ)-HIRED2(J))22,23,23
   23 I=9
      DATA(I)=DATA(I)+1.
      PUNCH 123,EMPNOD(NN)
  123 FORMAT(62H 9. EMPLOYE IMPROPERLY EXCLUDED FROM FICA RETURN, CLOCK
     1NUMBER,F5.0)
      CALL STTEST(I)
   22 JJ=1
  222 IF(EMPNO1(JJ)-EMPNO2(J))24,44,25
   24 JJ=JJ+1
      GO TO 222
   25 IF(TERMD2(J))44,44,26
   26 I=10
      DATA(I)=DATA(I)+1.
      PUNCH 126,EMPNOD(NN)
  126 FORMAT(73H 10.ERROR IN HIRING DATE ON MASTER PERSONNEL RECORD, EMP
     1LOYE CLOCK NUMBER,F5.0)
   44 RETURN
      END

      SUBROUTINE PAYNET(J,NN)
C     COMMON AND DIMENSION STATEMENTS DELETED
      EXMPN2(J)=EXMPN2(J)*13.0
      IF(EXMPN2(J)-GROSS(J))1,2,2
    1 WTHTAX(J)=(GROSS(J)-EXMPN2(J))*0.18
      GO TO 3
    2 WTHTAX(J)=0.0
    3 IF(YEART2(J)-4800.0)6,8,8
    6 YEART2(J)=YEART2(J)+GROSS(J)
      IF(YEART2(J)-4800.0)10,10,12
C     THERE IS A MAXIMUM LIMIT OF $4800.00 FOR COMPUTATION OF F.I.C.A. TAX
   12 FICA(J)=(GROSS(J)-(YEART2(J)-4800.0))*0.03
      GO TO 15
   10 FICA(J)=GROSS(J)*0.03
      GO TO 15
    8 FICA(J)=0.0
      YEART2(J)=GROSS(J)+YEART2(J)
   14 PYNET(J)=0.0
   15 PYNET(J)=GROSS(J)-WTHTAX(J)-FICA(J)
      RETURN
      END

      SUBROUTINE SORT2
C     COMMON AND DIMENSION STATEMENTS DELETED
      JJ=N-1
      DO 50 J=1,JJ
      II=II+1
      DO 50 J=II,N
      IF(AJOBN(I)-AJOBN(J))50,50,10
   10 TEMP=AJOBN(I)
      AJOBN(I)=AJOBN(J)
      AJOBN(J)=TEMP
      TEMP=DLLAR(I)
      DLLAR(I)=DLLAR(J)
      DLLAR(J)=TEMP
      TEMP=EMPNOD(I)
```

```
      EMPNOD(I)=EMPNOD(J)
      EMPNOD(J)=TEMP
   50 CONTINUE
   60 RETURN
      END

      SUBROUTINE EXCEPT(J,NN)
C     COMMON AND DIMENSION STATEMENTS DELETED
      II=1
    3 IF(EMPNBR(II)-EMPNO2(J))5,7,6
    5 II=II+1
      IF(II-LL)3,3,6
    6 IF(PYNET(J))50,50,66
   66 I=13
      DATA(I)=DATA(I)+1.
      PUNCH 16,EMPNO2(J),PYNET(J)
   16 FORMAT(57H 13.EMPLOYE WITH VALID TIME CARD WAS NOT PAID, CLOCK NO.
     1 ,F5.0,2H $,F6.2)
      CALL STTEST(I)
      GO TO 50
    7 IF(TAKHOM(II)-PYNET(J))20,50,10
   20 DIFF=PYNET(J)-TAKHOM(II)
      GO TO 15
   10 DIFF=TAKHOM(II)-PYNET(J)
   15 IF(DIFF-0.01)50,50,17
   17 PCENT=DIFF/PYNET(J)
      IF(PCENT-0.05)11,11,12
   11 I=15
      DATA(I)=DATA(I)+1.
      PUNCH 111,EMPNO2(J),DIFF
  111 FORMAT(60H 15.CALCULATED PAY DIFFERENCE LESS THAN 5 PERCENT, CLOCK
     1 NO.,F5.0,9H AMOUNT $,F6.2)
      CALL STTEST (I)
      GO TO 50
   12 I=14
      DATA(I)=DATA(I)+1.
      PUNCH 112,EMPNO2(J),DIFF
  112 FORMAT(60H 14.CALCULATED PAY DIFFERENCE MORE THAN 5 PERCENT, CLOCK
     1 NO.,F5.0,9H AMOUNT $,F6.2)
      CALL STTEST(I)
   50 RETURN
      END

      SUBROUTINE DSTRIB
C     COMMON AND DIMENSION STATEMENTS DELETED
      DO 50 J=1,N
      II=1
      SAMPNO=J
    1 IF(AJOBNU(II)-AJOBN(J))2,4,6
    2 II=II+1
      IF(II-KK)1,1,6
    6 IF(ABSF(DLLAR(J))-0.01)50,66,66
   66 I=11
      DATA(I)=DATA(I)+1.
      PUNCH 16,AJOBN(J),DLLAR(J),EMPNOD(J)
   16 FORMAT(27H 11.TIME TICKET FOR JOB NO.,F6.0,5H OF $,F6.2,24H NOT CH
     1ARGED, CLOCK NO. ,F5.0)
      CALL STTEST(I)
      GO TO 50
    4 TEMP=DOLLAR(II)-DLLAR(J)
```

```
      DOLLAR(II)=TEMP
   50 CONTINUE
      DO 100 J=1,KK
      SAMPNO=J
      IF(ABSF(DOLLAR(J))-0.01)100,12,12
   12 I=12
      DATA(I)=DATA(I)+1.
      PUNCH 111,AJOBNU(J),DOLLAR(J)
  111 FORMAT(38H 12.DISTRIBUTION ERROR FOR JOB NUMBER ,F5.0,5H OF $,F7.2
     1)
      CALL STTEST(I)
  100 CONTINUE
      SAMPNO=K
      RETURN
      END

      SUBROUTINE OVRVEW(J,NN)
C     COMMON AND DIMENSION STATEMENTS DELETED
      DO 10 I=1,15
      IF(DATA(I))2,2,4
    2 PUNCH 12,I
   12 FORMAT(54HOTEST PERIOD HAD NO ERRORS CLASSIFIED AS EXCEPTION NO.,I
     12)
      FINAL(I)=1.0
      GO TO 11
    4 PUNCH 14,I,DATA(I)
   14 FORMAT(15HOEXCEPTION NO. ,I2,9H OCCURRED,F4.0,6H TIMES)
      CALL STTEST(I)
   11 IF (REJECT(I))66,66,8
   66 IF (FINAL(I))6,6,88
    6 PUNCH 16,I
   16 FORMAT(56H ERROR RATE IS IN INDETERMINATE RANGE FOR EXCEPTION NO.
     1,I2)
      GO TO 10
    8 PUNCH 18,I
   18 FORMAT(64H ERROR RATE INDICATES THAT SAMPLE BE REJECTED FOR EXCEPT
     1ION NO. ,I2)
      GO TO 10
   88 PUNCH 80,I
   80 FORMAT(64H ERROR RATE INDICATES THAT SAMPLE BE ACCEPTED FOR EXCEPT
     1ION NO. ,I2)
   10 CONTINUE
   20 RETURN
      END

      SUBROUTINE GOOFRD(J,NN)
C     COMMON AND DIMENSION STATEMENTS DELETED
      IF(EMPNOD(NN)-EMPNO2(J))51,51,20
   20 II=1
   21 IF(EMPNO1(II)-EMPNO2(J))25,30,35
   25 II=II+1
      IF(II-M)21,21,35
   30 IF(TERMD1(II))35,35,44
   35 IF(TERMD2(J))38,38,44
   38 JJ=1
   37 IF(EMPNO3(JJ)-EMPNO2(J))40,42,44
   40 JJ=JJ+1
      IF(JJ-K)37,37,44
   42 IF(TERMD3(JJ))44,44,51
   44 II=1
```

```
    147 IF(EMPNO4(II)-EMPNO2(J))49,50,32
     49 II=II+1
        IF(II-KK)147,147,32
     50 IF(CHARGE(II)-1100.)55,51,55
     55 IF(CHARGE(II)-1200.)32,51,32
     32 JJ=1
     33 IF(EMPNBR(JJ)-EMPNO2(J))2,4,51
      2 JJ=JJ+1
        IF(JJ-LL)33,33,51
      4 PUNCH 444,EMPNO2(J),GRPAY(JJ)
    444 FORMAT(59H 1. TIME CARD IS MISSING BUT EMPLOYE WAS PAID,CLOCK NUMB
       1ER ,F5.0,9H AMOUNT $,F6.2)
        I=1
        DATA(I)=DATA(I)+1.
        CALL STTEST(I)
     51 NN=NN-1
        RETURN
        END

        SUBROUTINE STTEST(I)
C       COMMON AND DIMENSION STATEMENTS DELETED
        DATA(I)=DATA(I)+0.0001
        IF (INDEX(I))1,1,11
      1 P1(I)=HISTRY(I)-0.005
        P2(I)=HISTRY(I)+0.015
        IF(P1(I))5,5,6
      5 P1(I)=HISTRY(I)
C       COMPUTE H1,H2, AND S.
      6 H1(I)=LOGF(0.95/0.1)/(LOGF(P2(I)/P1(I))+LOGF((1.-P1(I))/(1.-P2(I))
       1))
        H2(I)=LOGF(0.9/0.05)/(LOGF(P2(I)/P1(I))+LOGF((1.-P1(I))/(1.-P2(I))
       1))
        S(I)=LOGF((1.-P1(I))/(1.-P2(I)))/(LOGF(P2(I)/P1(I))+LOGF((1.-P1(I)
       1)/(1.-P2(I))))
        INDEX(I)=1
        DA(I)=-H1(I)+S(I)*SAMPNO
        DR(I)=H2(I)+S(I)*SAMPNO
        GO TO 4
     11 IF(REJECT(I))2,2,50
      2 IF (FINAL(I))4,4,50
      4 DA(I)=-H1(I)+S(I)*SAMPNO
        DR(I)=H2(I)+S(I)*SAMPNO
     10 IF(DA(I))50,50,20
     20 IF(DA(I)-DATA(I))22,24,24
     22 IF(DR(I)-DATA(I))222,222,50
     24 PUNCH 124,I
    124 FORMAT(77H NUMBER OF EXCEPTIONS IN SAMPLE IS EQUAL TO OR LESS THAN
       1 ACCEPTABLE LIMIT FOR,I3)
        FINAL(I)=1.0
        GO TO 50
    222 PUNCH 126,I
    126 FORMAT(68H NUMBER OF EXCEPTIONS IN SAMPLE IS GREATER THAN ACCEPTAB
       1LE LIMIT FOR,I3)
        REJECT(I)=1.0
     50 DATA(I)=DATA(I)-0.0001
        RETURN
        END
```

```
C     SAMPLE OUTPUT FOLLOWS
SUMMARY OF EXCEPTIONS NOTED DURING THE TEST OF INTERNAL CONTROL
EXCEPTION NUMBERS ARE IDENTIFIED AS FOLLOWS.
 1.TIME CARD IS MISSING BUT EMPLOYE WAS PAID.
 2.MASTER CARD IS MISSING BUT EMPLOYE WAS NOT PAID.
 3.MASTER CARD IS MISSING, EMPLOYE WAS NOT PAID AND HE WAS IN LAST YEARS TEST.
 4.MASTER CARD IS MISSING, EMPLOYE WAS PAID AND HE WAS IN TEST PERIOD LAST YEAR.
 5.EMPLOYE IS CLASSIFIED IN THE WRONG DEPARTMENT.
 6.HASH TOTAL OF MASTER PERSONNEL FILE DOES NOT AGREE WITH PERSONNEL DEPT. COUNT
 7.OVERTIME PAID BUT IDLE TIME IS IN EXCESS OF 5 PERCENT.
 8.EXCESSIVE PAY RATE.
 9.EMPLOYE NOT ON F.I.C.A. RETURN.
10.ERROR IN HIRING DATE ON MASTER PAYROLL FILE.
11.TIME TICKET NOT CHARGED TO A JOB.
12.LABOR DISTRIBUTION ERROR.
13.EMPLOYE THAT WORKED DURING THE TEST PERIOD WAS NOT PAID.
14.ERROR IN NET PAY CALCULATION OF MORE THAN 5 PERCENT.
15.ERROR IN NET PAY CALCULATION LESS THAN 5 PERCENT.
EXCEPTION NO.  1 OCCURRED  1. TIMES
ERROR RATE IS IN INDETERMINATE RANGE FOR EXCEPTION NO.  1
EXCEPTION NO.  2 OCCURRED  6. TIMES
NUMBER OF EXCEPTIONS IN SAMPLE IS GREATER THAN ACCEPTABLE LIMIT FOR  2
ERROR RATE INDICATES THAT SAMPLE BE REJECTED FOR EXCEPTION NO.  2
TEST PERIOD HAD NO ERRORS CLASSIFIED AS EXCEPTION NO. 3
ERROR RATE INDICATES THAT SAMPLE BE ACCEPTED FOR EXCEPTION NO.  3
EXCEPTION NO.  4 OCCURRED  1. TIMES
ERROR RATE IS IN INDETERMINATE RANGE FOR EXCEPTION NO.  4
TEST PERIOD HAD NO ERRORS CLASSIFIED AS EXCEPTION NO. 5
ERROR RATE INDICATES THAT SAMPLE BE ACCEPTED FOR EXCEPTION NO.  5
EXCEPTION NO.  6 OCCURRED  1. TIMES
ERROR RATE IS IN INDETERMINATE RANGE FOR EXCEPTION NO.  6
TEST PERIOD HAD NO ERRORS CLASSIFIED AS EXCEPTION NO. 7
ERROR RATE INDICATES THAT SAMPLE BE ACCEPTED FOR EXCEPTION NO.  7
EXCEPTION NO.  8 OCCURRED 10. TIMES
NUMBER OF EXCEPTIONS IN SAMPLE IS GREATER THAN ACCEPTABLE LIMIT FOR  8
ERROR RATE INDICATES THAT SAMPLE BE REJECTED FOR EXCEPTION NO.  8
EXCEPTION NO.  9 OCCURRED  1. TIMES
ERROR RATE IS IN INDETERMINATE RANGE FOR EXCEPTION NO.  9
TEST PERIOD HAD NO ERRORS CLASSIFIED AS EXCEPTION NO.10
ERROR RATE INDICATES THAT SAMPLE BE ACCEPTED FOR EXCEPTION NO. 10
EXCEPTION NO. 11 OCCURRED  1. TIMES
NUMBER OF EXCEPTIONS IN SAMPLE IS EQUAL TO OR LESS THAN ACCEPTABLE LIMIT FOR 11
ERROR RATE INDICATES THAT SAMPLE BE ACCEPTED FOR EXCEPTION NO. 11
EXCEPTION NO. 12 OCCURRED  2. TIMES
NUMBER OF EXCEPTIONS IN SAMPLE IS EQUAL TO OR LESS THAN ACCEPTABLE LIMIT FOR 12
ERROR RATE INDICATES THAT SAMPLE BE ACCEPTED FOR EXCEPTION NO. 12
TEST PERIOD HAD NO ERRORS CLASSIFIED AS EXCEPTION NO.13
ERROR RATE INDICATES THAT SAMPLE BE ACCEPTED FOR EXCEPTION NO. 13
EXCEPTION NO. 14 OCCURRED 13. TIMES
NUMBER OF EXCEPTIONS IN SAMPLE IS GREATER THAN ACCEPTABLE LIMIT FOR 14
ERROR RATE INDICATES THAT SAMPLE BE REJECTED FOR EXCEPTION NO. 14
EXCEPTION NO. 15 OCCURRED  8. TIMES
NUMBER OF EXCEPTIONS IN SAMPLE IS GREATER THAN ACCEPTABLE LIMIT FOR 15
ERROR RATE INDICATES THAT SAMPLE BE REJECTED FOR EXCEPTION NO. 15

DETAIL OF EXCEPTIONS NOTED DURING TEST PERIOD FOR 150 EMPLOYES

 6. EMPLOYE HOURLY RATE HASH TOTAL DISAGREES WITH PERSONNEL DEPT.COUNT BY  0.005
 2. MASTER PERSONNEL RECORD IS MISSING BUT EMPLOYE WAS NOT PAID, CLOCK NO. 4114.
14.CALCULATED PAY DIFFERENCE MORE THAN 5 PERCENT, CLOCK NO.4121. AMOUNT $ 24.05
```

```
 2. MASTER PERSONNEL RECORD IS MISSING BUT EMPLOYE WAS NOT PAID, CLOCK NO. 4135.
 4. MASTER PERSONNEL RECORD IS MISSING, CLOCK NO. 4138. PAID $120.00
 8. HOURLY PAY RATE IS IN EXCESS OF UNION SCALE RATE $ 4.00 CLOCK NO. 4140.
15.CALCULATED PAY DIFFERENCE LESS THAN 5 PERCENT, CLOCK NO.4146. AMOUNT $  1.00
 8. HOURLY PAY RATE IS IN EXCESS OF UNION SCALE RATE $ 4.00 CLOCK NO. 4150.
14.CALCULATED PAY DIFFERENCE MORE THAN 5 PERCENT, CLOCK NO.4150. AMOUNT $ 12.64
15.CALCULATED PAY DIFFERENCE LESS THAN 5 PERCENT, CLOCK NO.4154. AMOUNT $  0.04
15.CALCULATED PAY DIFFERENCE LESS THAN 5 PERCENT, CLOCK NO.4155. AMOUNT $  0.80
14.CALCULATED PAY DIFFERENCE MORE THAN 5 PERCENT, CLOCK NO.4160. AMOUNT $  6.32
 8. HOURLY PAY RATE IS IN EXCESS OF UNION SCALE RATE $ 4.00 CLOCK NO. 4173.
 8. HOURLY PAY RATE IS IN EXCESS OF UNION SCALE RATE $ 4.00 CLOCK NO. 4175.
14.CALCULATED PAY DIFFERENCE MORE THAN 5 PERCENT, CLOCK NO.4177. AMOUNT $  7.22
14.CALCULATED PAY DIFFERENCE MORE THAN 5 PERCENT, CLOCK NO.4179. AMOUNT $ 25.28
15.CALCULATED PAY DIFFERENCE LESS THAN 5 PERCENT, CLOCK NO.4180. AMOUNT $  1.80
 8. HOURLY PAY RATE IS IN EXCESS OF UNION SCALE RATE $ 4.00 CLOCK NO. 4182.
14.CALCULATED PAY DIFFERENCE MORE THAN 5 PERCENT, CLOCK NO.4183. AMOUNT $  7.00
 2. MASTER PERSONNEL RECORD IS MISSING BUT EMPLOYE WAS NOT PAID, CLOCK NO. 4195.
14.CALCULATED PAY DIFFERENCE MORE THAN 5 PERCENT, CLOCK NO.4202. AMOUNT $ 24.05
 2. MASTER PERSONNEL RECORD IS MISSING BUT EMPLOYE WAS NOT PAID, CLOCK NO. 4216.
 8. HOURLY PAY RATE IS IN EXCESS OF UNION SCALE RATE $ 4.00 CLOCK NO. 4220.
15.CALCULATED PAY DIFFERENCE LESS THAN 5 PERCENT, CLOCK NO.4226. AMOUNT $  1.00
 8. HOURLY PAY RATE IS IN EXCESS OF UNION SCALE RATE $ 4.00 CLOCK NO. 4230.
14.CALCULATED PAY DIFFERENCE MORE THAN 5 PERCENT, CLOCK NO.4230. AMOUNT $ 12.64
15.CALCULATED PAY DIFFERENCE LESS THAN 5 PERCENT, CLOCK NO.4234. AMOUNT $  0.04
15.CALCULATED PAY DIFFERENCE LESS THAN 5 PERCENT, CLOCK NO.4235. AMOUNT $  0.80
 2. MASTER PERSONNEL RECORD IS MISSING BUT EMPLOYE WAS NOT PAID, CLOCK NO. 4238.
 1. TIME CARD IS MISSING BUT EMPLOYE WAS PAID,CLOCK NUMBER 4239. AMOUNT $132.00
14.CALCULATED PAY DIFFERENCE MORE THAN 5 PERCENT, CLOCK NO.4240. AMOUNT $  6.32
 9. EMPLOYE IMPROPERLY EXCLUDED FROM FICA RETURN, CLOCK NUMBER4252.
 8. HOURLY PAY RATE IS IN EXCESS OF UNION SCALE RATE $ 4.00 CLOCK NO. 4253.
 8. HOURLY PAY RATE IS IN EXCESS OF UNION SCALE RATE $ 4.00 CLOCK NO. 4255.
14.CALCULATED PAY DIFFERENCE MORE THAN 5 PERCENT, CLOCK NO.4257. AMOUNT $  7.22
14.CALCULATED PAY DIFFERENCE MORE THAN 5 PERCENT, CLOCK NO.4259. AMOUNT $ 25.28
15.CALCULATED PAY DIFFERENCE LESS THAN 5 PERCENT, CLOCK NO.4260. AMOUNT $  1.80
 8. HOURLY PAY RATE IS IN EXCESS OF UNION SCALE RATE $ 4.00 CLOCK NO. 4262.
14.CALCULATED PAY DIFFERENCE MORE THAN 5 PERCENT, CLOCK NO.4263. AMOUNT $  7.00
 2. MASTER PERSONNEL RECORD IS MISSING BUT EMPLOYE WAS NOT PAID, CLOCK NO. 4295.
14.CALCULATED PAY DIFFERENCE MORE THAN 5 PERCENT, CLOCK NO.4302. AMOUNT $ 24.05
REVIEW OF LABOR DISTRIBUTION PROCEDURE. IF NO COMMENT IS MADE, NO ERRORS NOTED
11.TIME TICKET FOR JOB NO. 4309. OF $120.00 NOT CHARGED, CLOCK NO. 4120.
12.DISTRIBUTION ERROR FOR JOB NUMBER 4406. OF $  0.01
12.DISTRIBUTION ERROR FOR JOB NUMBER 4409. OF $ 120.00
```

APPENDIX C

Computer Audit Program for the Test of an Order-billing System

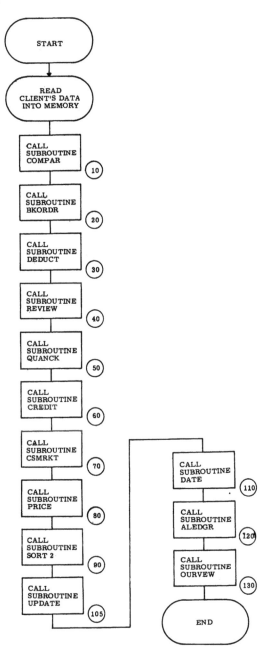

OVERALL BLOCK DIAGRAM
ORDER-PROCESSING MODEL

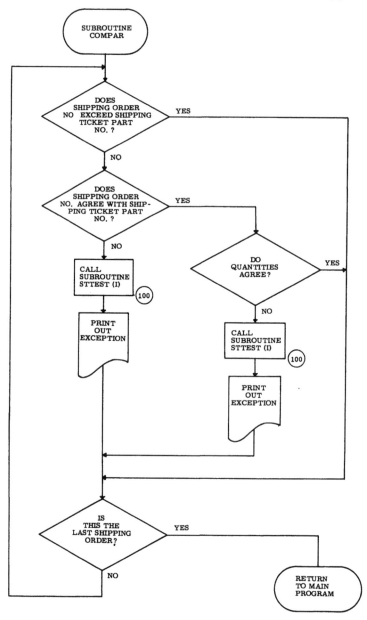

SUBROUTINE COMPAR - DETAIL (10)

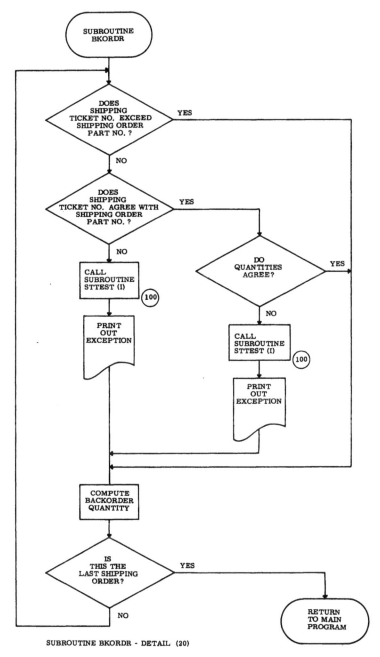

SUBROUTINE BKORDR - DETAIL (20)

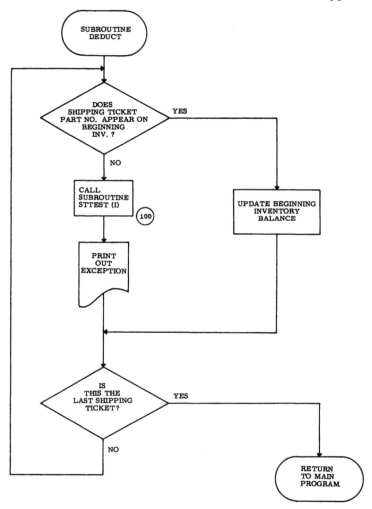

SUBROUTINE DEDUCT - DETAIL (30)

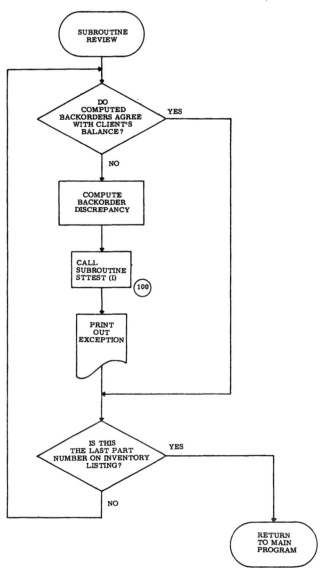

SUBROUTINE REVIEW - DETAIL (40)

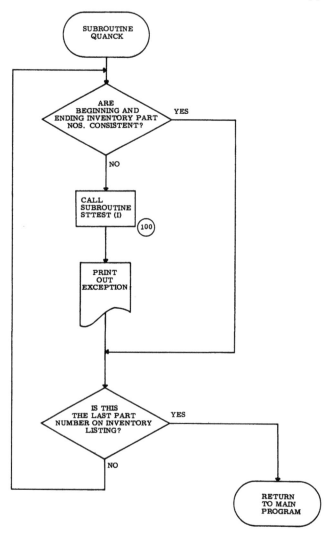

SUBROUTINE QUANCK - DETAIL (50)

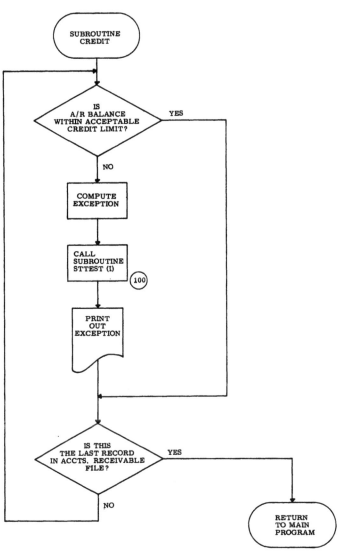

SUBROUTINE CREDIT - DETAIL (60)

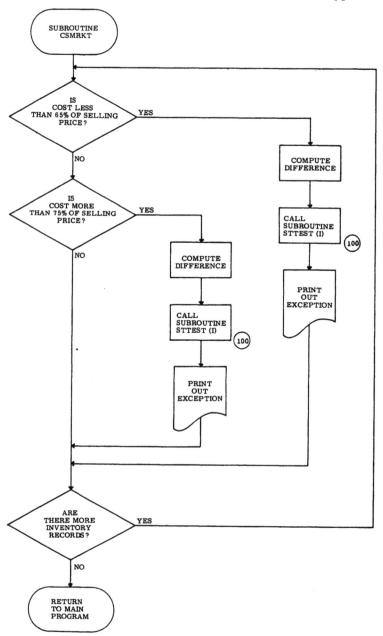

SUBROUTINE CSMRKT - DETAIL (70)

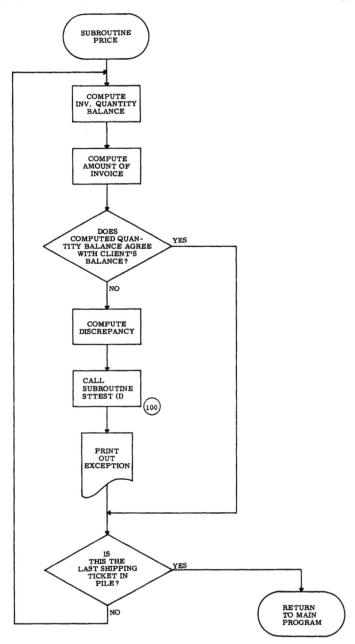

SUBROUTINE PRICE - DETAIL (80)

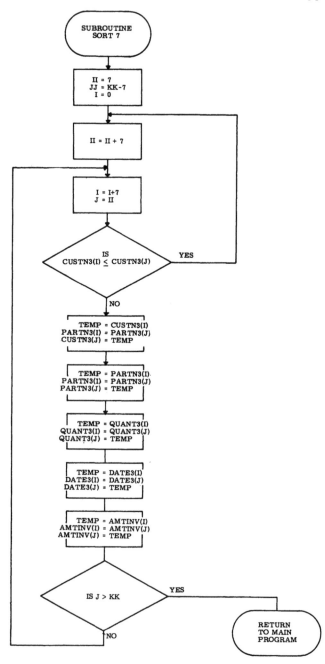

SUBROUTINE
SORT 7

II = 7
JJ = KK-7
I = 0

II = II + 7

I = I+7
J = II

IS
CUSTN3(I) ≤ CUSTN3(J)   YES

NO

TEMP = CUSTN3(I)
PARTN3(I) = PARTN3(J)
CUSTN3(J) = TEMP

TEMP = PARTN3(I)
PARTN3(I) = PARTN3(J)
PARTN3(J) = TEMP

TEMP = QUANT3(I)
QUANT3(I) = QUANT3(J)
QUANT3(J) = TEMP

TEMP = DATE3(I)
DATE3(I) = DATE3(J)
DATE3(J) = TEMP

TEMP = AMTINV(I)
AMTINV(I) = AMTINV(J)
AMTINV(J) = TEMP

IS J > KK   YES

NO

RETURN
TO MAIN
PROGRAM

SUBROUTINE SORT 2 - DETAIL (90)

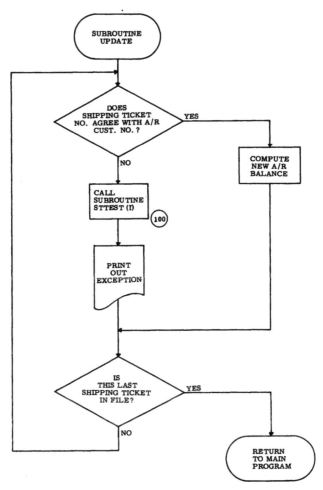

SUBROUTINE UPDATE - DETAIL (105)

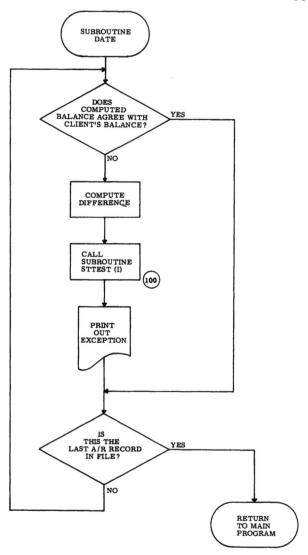

SUBROUTINE DATE - DETAIL (110)

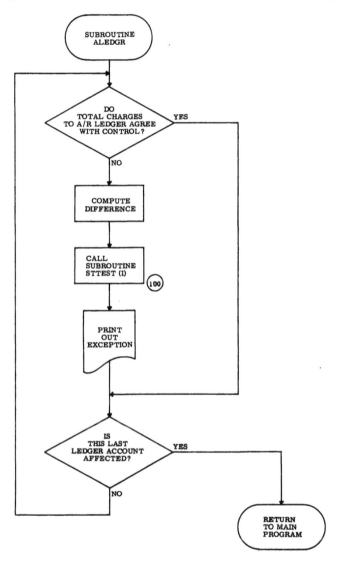

SUBROUTINE ALEDGR - DETAIL (120)

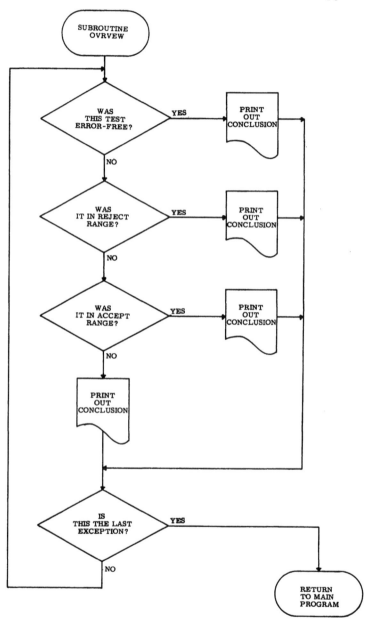

SUBROUTINE OVRVEW - DETAIL (130)

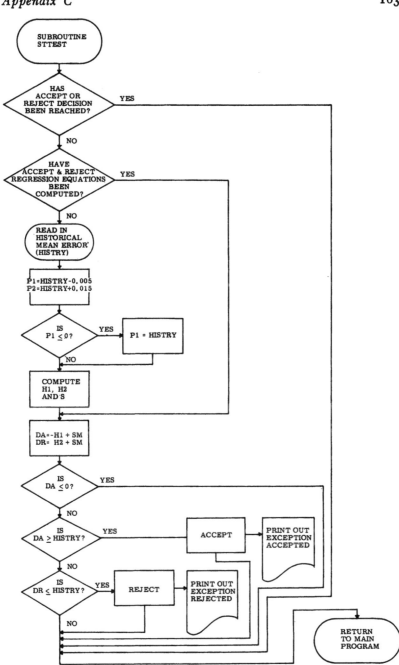

SUBROUTINE
STTEST

HAS
ACCEPT OR
REJECT DECISION
BEEN REACHED? — YES

NO

HAVE
ACCEPT & REJECT
REGRESSION EQUATIONS
BEEN
COMPUTED? — YES

NO

READ IN
HISTORICAL
MEAN ERROR'
(HISTRY)

P1=HISTRY-0.005
P2=HISTRY+0.015

IS
P1 $\leq$ 0? — YES → P1 = HISTRY

NO

COMPUTE
H1, H2
AND S

DA=-H1 + SM
DR= H2 + SM

IS
DA $\leq$ 0? — YES

NO

IS
DA $\geq$ HISTRY? — YES → ACCEPT → PRINT OUT
EXCEPTION
ACCEPTED

NO

IS
DR $\leq$ HISTRY? — YES → REJECT → PRINT OUT
EXCEPTION
REJECTED

NO

RETURN
TO MAIN
PROGRAM

Sequential sampling equations adapted from: R. M. and H. Justin Davidson, Statistical
Sampling for Accounting Information (Englewood Cliffs, N. J., 1962, Prentice-Hall,
Inc.), pp. 163-165.

SUBROUTINE STTEST - DETAIL (100)

```
                    MAIN ORDER PROCESSING PROGRAM
        COMMON K,L,M,N,KK,LL,PARTN1,PRICE1,ORDPT1,QUANT1,UNIT1,AMONT1,BAKO
       1R1,SELPR1,PARTN2,PRICE2,ORDPT2,QUANT2,UNIT2,AMONT2,BAKOR2,SELPR2,C
       2USTN1,BAL301,BAL601,BAL901,TOTAL1,CRLIM1,CUSTN2,BAL302,BAL602,BAL9
       302,TOTAL2,CRLIM2,CUSTN3,PARTN3,QUANT3,DATE3,CUSTN4,PARTN4,QUANT4,D
       4ATE4,ACCREC,SALES1,SALES2,SALES3,SALES4,CRLIMT,DATA,AMTINV,REJECT,
       5FINAL,HISTRY,INDEX,SAMPNO
        DIMENSION PARTN1(300),PRICE1(300),ORDPT1(300),QUANT1(300),UNIT1(30
       10),AMONT1(300),BAKOR1(300),SELPR1(300),PARTN2(300),PRICE2(300),ORD
       2PT2(300),QUANT2(300),UNIT2(300),AMONT2(300),BAKOR2(300),SELPR2(300
       3),CUSTN1(300),BAL301(300),BAL601(300),BAL901(300),TOTAL1(300),CRLI
       4M1(300),CUSTN2(300),BAL302(300),BAL602(300),BAL902(300),TOTAL2(300
       5),CRLIM2(300),CUSTN3(500),PARTN3(500),QUANT3(500),DATE3(500),CUSTN
       64(500),PARTN4(500),QUANT4(500),DATE4(500),ACCREC(2),SALES1(2),SALE
       7S2(2),SALES3(2),SALES4(2),DATA(30),AMTINV(500),REJECT(20),FINAL(20
       8),HISTRY(20),INDEX(20),H1(20),H2(20),P1(20),P2(20),S(20),DA(20),DR
       9(20)
        READ 1,K,L,M,N,KK,LL
      1 FORMAT(6I3)
        READ 2,(PARTN1(J),PRICE1(J),ORDPT1(J),QUANT1(J),UNIT1(J),AMONT1(J)
       1,BAKOR1(J),SELPR1(J),J=1,K)
      2 FORMAT(F4.0,F7.2,2F5.0,F3.0,F7.2,F5.0,F7.2)
        READ 2,(PARTN2(J),PRICE2(J),ORDPT2(J),QUANT2(J),UNIT2(J),AMONT2(J)
       1,BAKOR2(J),SELPR2(J),J=1,L)
        READ 4,(CUSTN1(J),BAL301(J),BAL601(J),BAL901(J),TOTAL1(J),CRLIM1(J
       1),J=1,M)
        READ 4,(CUSTN2(J),BAL302(J),BAL602(J),BAL902(J),TOTAL2(J),CRLIM2(J
       1),J=1,N)
      4 FORMAT(F4.0,5F8.2)
        READ 6,(CUSTN3(J),PARTN3(J),QUANT3(J),DATE3(J),J=1,KK)
        READ 6,(CUSTN4(J),PARTN4(J),QUANT4(J),DATE4(J),J=1,LL)
      6 FORMAT(3F5.0,F6.0)
C     K IS THE NUMBER OF RECORDS IN BEGINNING INVENTORY FILE)
C     L IS THE NUMBER OF RECORDS IN ENDING INVENTORY FILE.
C     M IS THE NUMBER OF RECORDS IN BEGINNING A/R FILE
C     N IS THE NUMBER OF RECORDS IN ENDING A/R FILE
C     KK IS THE NUMBER OF SHIPPING TICKETS DURING THE TEST PERIOD.
C     LL IS THE NUMBER OF SHIPPING ORDERS PROCESSED DURING THE TEST PERIOD.
        READ 8,(ACCREC(J),SALES1(J),SALES2(J),SALES3(J),SALES4(J),J=1,2)
      8 FORMAT(5F10.2)
C     1 IS THE OPENING BALANCE AND 2 IS THE CLOSING BALANCE.
        PUNCH 10,KK
     10 FORMAT(62H1DETAIL OF EXCEPTIONS NOTED DURING THE TEST PERIOD COMPR
       1ISING ,I3,16H SHIPPING ORDERS//)
C     THE OUTPUT TAPE IS LABELED
        READ 12,(HISTRY(I),I=1,15)
        READ 12,(FINAL(I),I=1,15)
        READ 12,(REJECT(I),I=1,15)
     12 FORMAT(F4.3)
C     ALL THE DATA ARE IN.
        CALL COMPAR
        CALL BKORDR
        CALL DEDUCT
        CALL REVIEW
        CALL QUANCK
        CALL CREDIT
        CALL CSMRKT
        CALL PRICE
        CALL SORT1
        CALL UPDATE
```

```
      CALL DATE
      CALL ALEDGR
      PUNCH 14
      PUNCH 15
   14 FORMAT(64H1SUMMARY OF EXCEPTIONS NOTED DURING THE TEST OF INTERNAL
     1 CONTROL/44HEXCEPTION NUMBERS ARE IDENTIFIED AS FOLLOWS./38H 1. IN
     2DICATES SHIPMENTS EXCEED ORDERS./36H 2.INDICATES UNAUTHORIZED SHIP
     3MENTS./37H 3.INDICATES ORDERS EXCEED SHIPMENTS./30H 4.INDICATES UN
     4SHIPPED ORDERS./39H 5.ITEM NOT LISTED IN ENDING INVENTORY./43H 6.I
     5TEM SHIPPED NOT IN BEGINNING INVENTORY./25H 7.BACKORDER DISCREPANC
     6Y./47H 8.DIFFERENCES IN BEGINNING OR ENDING PART NOS./37H 9.ENDING
     7 INVENTORY BALANCE IN ERROR./42H 10.ACCTS. RECEIVABLE EXCEED CREDI
     8T LIMIT./47H 11.COST LESS THAN 65 PERCENT OF SELLING PRICE./45H 12
     9.LOWER OF COST OR MARKET RULE IS VIOLATED.)
   15 FORMAT(45H 13.ITEM SHIPPED BUT NOT CHARGED TO CUSTOMER./44H 14.ACC
     1OUNTS RECEIVABLE BALANCE DISCREPANCY./65H 15.DEBITS TO A/R LEDGER
     2DO NOT AGREE WITH GENERAL LEDGER TOTALS.)
      CALL OVRVEW
C     WE ARE DONE
      CALL EXIT
      END

      SUBROUTINE COMPAR
C     COMMON AND DIMENSION STATEMENTS DELETED
      JJ=1
      J=0
   10 J=J+1
      SAMPNO=J
      IF(J-LL)1,1,60
    1 IF(PARTN4(J)-PARTN3(JJ))50,2,6
    2 IF(QUANT4(J)-QUANT3(JJ))4,40,40
    4 SUM=QUANT3(JJ)-QUANT4(J)
      I=1
      DATA(I)=DATA(I)+1.
      PUNCH 14,SUM,PARTN3(JJ)
   14 FORMAT(31H 1. SHIPMENTS EXCEED ORDERS BY ,F6.0,12H FOR PART NO.,F5
     1.0)
      CALL STTEST(I)
      GO TO 40
    6 I=2
      DATA(I)=DATA(I)+1.
      PUNCH 16,QUANT3(JJ),PARTN3(JJ)
   16 FORMAT(27H 2. UNAUTHORIZED SHIPMENT OF,F6.0,18HITEMS FOR PART NO.,
     1F5.0)
      CALL STTEST(I)
   40 JJ=JJ+1
      IF(JJ-KK)10,10,60
   50 GO TO 10
   60 RETURN
      END

      SUBROUTINE BKORDR
C     COMMON AND DIMENSION STATEMENTS DELETED
      J=1
      JJ=0
      II=1
   10 JJ=JJ+1
      SAMPNO=J
    1 IF(PARTN3(JJ)-PARTN4(J))11,2,6
   11 IF(JJ-KK)10,6,6
```

```
    2 IF(QUANT3(JJ)-QUANT4(J))4,40,40
    4 DIFR=QUANT4(J)-QUANT3(JJ)
      I=3
      DATA(I)=DATA(I)+1.
      PUNCH 14,DIFR,PARTN4(J)
   14 FORMAT(31H 3. ORDERS EXCEED SHIPMENTS BY ,F6.0,12HFOR PART NO.,F5.
     10)
      CALL STTEST(I)
      GO TO 30
    6 I=4
      DATA(I)=DATA(I)+1.
      PUNCH 16,QUANT4(J),PARTN4(J)
   16 FORMAT(22H 4. UNSHIPPED ORDER OF,F6.0,19H ITEMS FOR PART NO.,F5.0)
      JJ=JJ-1
      DIFR=QUANT4(J)
      CALL STTEST(I)
   30 IF(PARTN2(II)-PARTN4(J))31,32,33
   31 II=II+1
      IF(II-L)30,30,33
   32 BAKOR2(II)=BAKOR2(II) - DIFR
      GO TO 40
   33 I=5
      DATA(I)=DATA(I)+1.
      PUNCH 133,PARTN4(J)
  133 FORMAT(16H 5. PART NUMBER ,F5.0,31H NOT LISTED IN ENDING INVENTORY
     1)
      CALL STTEST(I)
   40 J=J+1
      IF(J-LL)10,10,60
   60 RETURN
      END


      SUBROUTINE DEDUCT
C     COMMON AND DIMENSION STATEMENTS DELETED
      II=1
      J=0
   10 J=J+1
      SAMPNO=J
      IF(J-KK)12,12,30
   12 IF(PARTN1(II)-PARTN3(J))14,16,20
   14 II=II+1
      IF(II-K)12,12,30
   16 QUANT1(II)=QUANT1(II)-QUANT3(J)
      GO TO 10
   20 I=6
      DATA(I)=DATA(I)+1.
      PUNCH 21,PARTN3(J),QUANT3(J)
   21 FORMAT(39H 6. FILE INDICATES SHIPMENT OF PART NO., F6.0,3H OF,F5.0
     1,23H UNITS NOT IN INVENTORY)
      CALL STTEST(I)
      GO TO 10
   30 RETURN
      END


      SUBROUTINE REVIEW
C     COMMON AND DIMENSION STATEMENTS DELETED
      II=1
      SAMPNO=0.0
    5 IF(BAKOR2(II))10,30,20
   10 SAMPNO=II
```

```
      I=7
      BAKOR2(II)= -BAKOR2(II)
      DATA(I)=DATA(I)+1.
      PUNCH 11,PARTN2(II),BAKOR2(II)
   11 FORMAT(61H 7. COMPUTED BACKORDERS EXCEED TOTAL BACKORDERS FOR PART
     1 NO. ,F5.0,3H BY,F5.0,6H UNITS)
      CALL STTEST(I)
      GO TO 30
   20 SAMPNO=II
      I=7
      DATA(I)=DATA(I)+1.
      PUNCH 21,PARTN2(II),BAKOR2(II)
   21 FORMAT(61H 7. TOTAL BACKORDERS EXCEED COMPUTED BACKORDERS FOR PART
     1 NO. ,F5.0,3H BY,F5.0,6H UNITS)
      CALL STTEST(I)
   30 II=II+1
      IF(II-L)5,5,50
   50 RETURN
      END


      SUBROUTINE QUANCK
C     COMMON AND DIMENSION STATEMENTS DELETED
      II=1
      J=0
   10 J=J+1
      SAMPNO=J
      IF(J-L)15,15,50
   15 IF(PARTN1(II)-PARTN2(J))20,11,30
   20 I=8
      DATA(I)=DATA(I)+1.
      PUNCH 21,PARTN1(II),QUANT1(II),AMONT1(II)
   21 FORMAT(13H 8. PART NO. ,F5.0,34H NOT ON ENDING INVENTORY, QUANTITY
     1,F6.0,2H $,F8.2)
      CALL STTEST(I)
      II=II+1
      IF(II-K)15,15,50
   30 I=8
      DATA(I)=DATA(I)+1.
      PUNCH 31,PARTN2(J),QUANT2(J)
   31 FORMAT(13H 8. PART NO. ,F5.0,37H NOT ON BEGINNING INVENTORY, QUANT
     1ITY,F6.0,2H $,F8.2)
      CALL STTEST(I)
      GO TO 10
   11 II=II+1
      IF(II-K)10,10,50
   50 RETURN
      END


      SUBROUTINE CREDIT
C     COMMON AND DIMENSION STATEMENTS DELETED
      DO 50 J=1,N
      SAMPNO=J
      IF(TOTAL2(J)-CRLIM2(J))50,50,10
   10 I=10
      DATA(I)=DATA(I)+1.
      PUNCH 12,TOTAL2(J),CRLIM2(J),CUSTN2(J)
   12 FORMAT(30H 10.ACCT. RECEIVABLE BALANCE $,F8.2,15H CREDIT LIMIT $,F
     18.2,14H FOR CUST. NO.,F5.0)
      CALL STTEST(I)
   50 CONTINUE
```

```
      CALL STTEST(I)
      GO TO 50
   40 PUNCH 45,DIFFER
   45 FORMAT(50H 15.DETAIL CHARGES EXCEED A/R CONTROL AMOUNTS BY $,F8.2)
      I=15
      DATA(I)=DATA(I)+1.
      CALL STTEST(I)
   50 RETURN
      END


      SUBROUTINE STTEST(I)
C     COMMON AND DIMENSION STATEMENTS DELETED
      DATA(I)=DATA(I)+0.0001
      IF (INDEX(I))1,1,11
    1 P1(I)=HISTRY(I)-0.005
      P2(I)=HISTRY(I)+0.015
      IF(P1(I))5,5,6
    5 P1(I)=HISTRY(I)
C     COMPUTE H1,H2, AND S.
    6 H1(I)=LOGF(0.95/0.1)/(LOGF(P2(I)/P1(I))+LOGF((1.-P1(I))/(1.-P2(I))
     1))
      H2(I)=LOGF(0.9/0.05)/(LOGF(P2(I)/P1(I))+LOGF((1.-P1(I))/(1.-P2(I))
     1))
      S(I)=LOGF((1.-P1(I))/(1.-P2(I)))/(LOGF(P2(I)/P1(I))+LOGF((1.-P1(I)
     1)/(1.-P2(I))))
      INDEX(I)=1
      DA(I)=-H1(I)+S(I)*SAMPNO
      DR(I)=H2(I)+S(I)*SAMPNO
      GO TO 4
   11 IF(REJECT(I))2,2,50
    2 IF (FINAL(I))4,4,50
    4 DA(I)=-H1(I)+S(I)*SAMPNO
      DR(I)=H2(I)+S(I)*SAMPNO
   10 IF(DA(I))50,50,20
   20 IF(DA(I)-DATA(I))22,24,24
   22 IF(DR(I)-DATA(I))222,222,50
   24 PUNCH 124,I
  124 FORMAT(77H NUMBER OF EXCEPTIONS IN SAMPLE IS EQUAL TO OR LESS THAN
     1 ACCEPTABLE LIMIT FOR,I3)
      FINAL(I)=1.0
      GO TO 50
  222 PUNCH 126,I
  126 FORMAT(68H NUMBER OF EXCEPTIONS IN SAMPLE IS GREATER THAN ACCEPTAB
     1LE LIMIT FOR,I3)
      REJECT(I)=1.0
   50 DATA(I)=DATA(I)-0.0001
      RETURN
      END


C     SAMPLE OUTPUT FOLLOWS
```

SUMMARY OF EXCEPTIONS NOTED DURING THE TEST OF INTERNAL CONTROL
EXCEPTIONS NUMBERS ARE IDENTIFIED AS FOLLOWS.
1. INDICATES SHIPMENTS EXCEED ORDERS.
2. INDICATES UNAUTHORIZED SHIPMENTS.
3. INDICATES ORDERS EXCEED SHIPMENTS.
4. INDICATES UNSHIPPED ORDERS.
5. ITEM NOT LISTED IN ENDING INVENTORY.
6. ITEM SHIPPED NOT IN BEGINNING INVENTORY.
7. BACKORDER DISCREPANCY.
8. DIFFERENCES IN BEGINNING OR ENDING PART NOS.

```
  100 CONTINUE
      CALL STTEST(I)
      RETURN
      END

      SUBROUTINE SORT1
C     COMMON AND DIMENSION STATEMENTS DELETED
      JJ=KK-1
      DO 50 I=1,JJ
      II=II+1
      DO 50 J=II,KK
      IF(CUSTN3(I)-CUSTN3(J))50,50,10
   10 TEMP=CUSTN3(I)
      CUSTN3(I)=CUSTN3(J)
      CUSTN3(J)=TEMP
      TEMP=PARTN3(I)
      PARTN3(I)=PARTN3(J)
      PARTN3(J)=TEMP
      TEMP=QUANT3(I)
      QUANT3(I)=QUANT3(J)
      QUANT3(J)=TEMP
      TEMP=DATE3(I)
      DATE3(I)=DATE3(J)
      DATE3(J)=TEMP
      TEMP=AMTINV(I)
      AMTINV(I)=AMTINV(J)
      AMTINV(J)=TEMP
   50 CONTINUE
   60 RETURN
      END

      SUBROUTINE UPDATE
C     COMMON AND DIMENSION STATEMENTS DELETED
      II=1
      DO 100 J=1,KK
      SAMPNO=J
    1 IF(CUSTN2(II)-CUSTN3(J))2,4,6
    2 II=II+1
      IF(II-N)1,1,6
    6 I=13
      DATA(I)=DATA(I)+1.
      PUNCH 116,CUSTN3(J),AMTINV(J)
  116 FORMAT(28H 13.SHIPMENT TO CUSTOMER NO.,F5.0,33H NOT POSTED TO A/R
     1FILE,AMOUNT $,F8.2)
      CALL STTEST(I)
      GO TO 50
    4 BAL302(II)=BAL302(II)-AMTINV(J)
   50 II=1
  100 CONTINUE
  200 RETURN
      END

      SUBROUTINE DATE
C     COMMON AND DIMENSION STATEMENTS DELETED
      DO 100 J=1,N
      SAMPNO=J
      IF(BAL302(J)-0.01)110,10,10
  110 ADD= -0.01
      IF(BAL302(J)-ADD)10,10,100
   10 IF(BAL302(J))5,100,7
```

```
  5 DIFFER=BAL302(J)*(-1.)
    I=14
    DATA(I)=DATA(I)+1.
    PUNCH 121,CUSTN2(J),DIFFER
121 FORMAT(61H 14.COMPUTED ENDING A/R BALANCE EXCEEDS BALANCE FOR CUST
   1. NO.,F5.0,5H BY $,F8.2)
    GO TO 100
  7 DIFFER=BAL302(J)
    I=14
    DATA(I)=DATA(I)+1.
    PUNCH 122,CUSTN2(J),DIFFER
122 FORMAT(61H 14.BALANCE EXCEEDS COMPUTED ENDING A/R BALANCE FOR CUST
   1. NO.,F5.0,5H BY $,F8.2)
100 CONTINUE
    CALL STTEST(I)
    RETURN
    END

    SUBROUTINE OVRVEW
C   COMMON AND DIMENSION STATEMENTS DELETED
    DO 10 I=1,15
    IF(DATA(I))2,2,4
  2 PUNCH 12,I
 12 FORMAT(54HOTEST PERIOD HAD NO ERRORS CLASSIFIED AS EXCEPTION NO.,I
   12)
    FINAL(I)=1.0
    GO TO 11
  4 PUNCH 14,I,DATA(I)
 14 FORMAT(14HOEXCEPTION NO.,I2,9H OCCURRED,F3.0,6H TIMES)
 11 IF (REJECT(I))66,66,8
 66 IF (FINAL(I))6,6,88
  6 PUNCH 16,I
 16 FORMAT(56H ERROR RATE IS IN INDETERMINATE RANGE FOR EXCEPTION NO.
   1,I2)
    GO TO 10
  8 PUNCH 18,I
 18 FORMAT(64H ERROR RATE INDICATES THAT SAMPLE BE REJECTED FOR EXCEPT
   1ION NO. ,I2)
    GO TO 10
 88 PUNCH 80,I
 80 FORMAT(64H ERROR RATE INDICATES THAT SAMPLE BE ACCEPTED FOR EXCEPT
   1ION NO. ,I2)
 10 CONTINUE
 20 RETURN
    END

    SUBROUTINE ALEDGR
    COMMON K,L,M,N,KK,LL,PARTN1,PRICE1,ORDPT1,QUANT1,UNIT1,AMONT1,BAKO
    SUM=0.0
    DO 10 J=1,N
 10 SUM=BAL302(J)+SUM
    DIFFER=SUM-ACCREC(2)
    IF(ABSF(DIFFER)-0.01)50,20,20
 20 IF(DIFFER)30,30,40
 30 DIFFER= -DIFFER
    PUNCH 35,DIFFER
 35 FORMAT(63H 15.DEBITS POSTED TO CONTROL ACCOUNT EXCEED DETAIL AMOUN
   1TS BY $,F8.2)
    I=15
    DATA(I)=DATA(I)+1.
```

```
      CALL STTEST(I)
      RETURN
      END

      SUBROUTINE CSMRKT
C     COMMON AND DIMENSION STATEMENTS DELETED
      J=0
   10 J=J+1
      SAMPNO=J
      DIVIS=PRICE2(J)/SELPR2(J)
      IF(DIVIS-0.65)2,4,4
    4 IF(DIVIS-0.75)45,45,6
    2 I=11
      DATA(I)=DATA(I)+1.
      PUNCH 12,DIVIS,PARTN2(J),AMONT2(J)
   12 FORMAT(12H 11.COST IS ,F4.3,39H PERCENT OF SELLING PRICE FOR PART
     1NO. ,F5.0,8H VALUE $,F8.2)
      CALL STTEST(I)
      GO TO 45
    6 I=12
      DATA(I)=DATA(I)+1.
      PUNCH 112,DIVIS,PARTN2(J),AMONT2(J)
  112 FORMAT(12H 11.COST IS ,F4.3,39H PERCENT OF SELLING PRICE FOR PART
     1NO. ,F5.0,8H VALUE $,F8.2)
      CALL STTEST(I)
   45 IF(J-L)10,50,50
   50 RETURN
      END

      SUBROUTINE PRICE
C     COMMON AND DIMENSION STATEMENTS DELETED
      DO 50 J=1,KK
      II=1
    1 IF(PARTN1(II)-PARTN3(J))2,4,50
    2 II=II+1
      IF(II-K)1,1,50
    4 AMTINV(J)=SELPR1(II)*QUANT3(J)
   50 CONTINUE
      DO 100 J=1,L
      II=1
      SAMPNO=J
   11 IF(PARTN1(II)-PARTN2(J))22,44,100
   22 II=II+1
      IF(II-K)11,11,100
   44 TTT=QUANT1(II)-QUANT2(J)
C     TTT IS QUANTITY ERROR IN ENDING INVENTORY
      IF(ABSF(TTT)-1.0)100,55,55
   55 I=9
      DATA(I)=DATA(I)+1.
      DDD=TTT*PRICE2(J)
C     DDD IS COMPUTED DOLLAR VALUE OF ENDING INVENTORY ERROR
      IF(DDD)66,100,77
   66 DDD= -DDD
      TTT= -TTT
      PUNCH 666,PARTN2(J),TTT,DDD
  666 FORMAT(39H 9. ENDING INVENTORY ERROR FOR PART NO.,F5.0,4H OF ,F5.0
     1,8H UNITS $,F8.2)
      GO TO 88
   77 PUNCH 666,PARTN2(J),TTT,DDD
   88 CALL STTEST(I)
```

9.ENDING INVENTORY BALANCE IN ERROR.
10.ACCTS. RECEIVABLE EXCEED CREDIT LIMIT.
11.COST LESS THAN 65 PERCENT OF SELLING PRICE.
12.LOWER OF COST OR MARKET RULE IS VIOLATED.
13.ITEM SHIPPED BUT NOT CHARGED TO CUSTOMER.
14.ACCOUNTS RECEIVABLE BALANCE DISCREPANCY.
15.DEBITS TO A/R LEDGER DO NOT AGREE WITH GENERAL LEDGER TOTALS.
EXCEPTION NO. 1 OCCURRED 2. TIMES
ERROR RATE IS IN INDETERMINATE RANGE FOR EXCEPTION NO. 1
EXCEPTION NO. 2. OCCURRED 1. TIMES
ERROR RATE IS IN INDETERMINATE RANGE FOR EXCEPTION NO. 2
EXCEPTION NO. 3 OCCURRED 2. TIMES
ERROR RATE IS IN INDETERMINATE RANGE FOR EXCEPTION NO. 3
EXCEPTION NO. 4 OCCURRED 1. TIMES
ERROR RATE IS IN INDETERMINATE RANGE FOR EXCEPTION NO. 4
TEST PERIOD HAD NO ERRORS CLASSIFIED AS EXCEPTION NO. 5
ERROR RATE INDICATES THAT SAMPLE BE ACCEPTED FOR EXCEPTION NO. 5
EXCEPTION NO. 6 OCCURRED 1. TIMES
ERROR RATE IS IN INDETERMINATE RANGE FOR EXCEPTION NO. 6
EXCEPTION NO. 7 OCCURRED 3. TIMES
ERROR RATE IS IN INDETERMINATE RANGE FOR EXCEPTION NO. 7
EXCEPTION NO. 8 OCCURRED 1. TIMES
ERROR RATE IS IN INDETERMINATE RANGE FOR EXCEPTION NO. 8
EXCEPTION NO. 9 OCCURRED17. TIMES
ERROR RATE INDICATES THAT SAMPLE BE REJECTED FOR EXCEPTION NO. 9
EXCEPTION NO.10 OCCURRED12. TIMES
ERROR RATE INDICATES THAT SAMPLE BE REJECTED FOR EXCEPTION NO. 10
EXCEPTION NO.11 OCCURRED 12. TIMES
ERROR RATE INDICATES THAT SAMPLE BE REJECTED FOR EXCEPTION NO. 11
EXCEPTION NO.12 OCCURED 4. TIMES
ERROR RATE IS IN INDETERMINATE RANGE FOR EXCEPTION NO. 12
TEST PERIOD HAD NO ERRORS CLASSIFIED AS EXCEPTION NO.13
ERROR RATE INDICATES THAT SAMPLE BE ACCEPTED FOR EXCEPTION NO. 13
EXCEPTION NO.14 OCCURRED14. TIMES
ERROR RATE INDICATES THAT SAMPLE BE REJECTED FOR EXCEPTION NO. 14
EXCEPTION NO.15 OCCURRED 1. TIMES
ERROR RATE IS IN INDETERMINATE RANGE FOR EXCEPTION NO. 15

DETAIL OF EXCEPTIONS NOTED DURING THE TEST PERIOD COMPRISING 279 SHIPPING ORDERS

1. SHIPMENTS EXCEED ORDERS BY   999. FOR PART NO1129.
1. SHIPMENTS EXCEED ORDERS BY   1. FOR PART NO5129.
2. UNAUTHORIZED SHIPMENT O 4999.ITEMS FOR PART NO.5129.
3. ORDERS EXCEED SHIPMENTS BY   3.FOR PART NO.1100.
3. ORDERS EXCEED SHIPMENTS BY   1.FOR PART NO.1111.
4. UNSHIPPED ORDER OF   6. ITEMS FOR PART NO.4002.
6. FILE INDICATES SHIPMENT OF PART NO. 3001. OF   4. UNITS NOT IN INVENTORY
7. COMPUTED BACKORDERS EXCEED TOTAL BACKORDERS FOR PART NO. 1100. BY   3. UNITS
7. COMPUTED BACKORDERS EXCEED TOTAL BACKORDERS FOR PART NO. 1111. BY   1. UNITS
7. COMPUTED BACKORDERS EXCEED TOTAL BACKORDERS FOR PART NO. 4002. BY   6. UNITS
8. PART NO. 3001. NOT ON BEGINNING INVENTORY. QUANTITY   46. $ 92.00
10.ACCT. RECEIVABLE BALANCE $ 1915.00 CREDIT LIMIT $ 1000.00 FOR CUST. NO.2101.
10.ACCT. RECEIVABLE BALANCE $ 3575.00 CREDIT LIMIT $ 2000.00 FOR CUST. NO.2102.
10.ACCT. RECEIVABLE BALANCE $ 1070.00 CREDIT LIMIT $ 500.00 FOR CUST. NO.2103.
10.ACCT. RECEIVABLE BALANCE $ 1915.00 CREDIT LIMIT $ 1000.00 FOR CUST. NO.3101.
10.ACCT. RECEIVABLE BALANCE $ 3575.00 CREDIT LIMIT $ 2000.00 FOR CUST. NO.3102.
10.ACCT. RECEIVABLE BALANCE $ 1070.00 CREDIT LIMIT $ 500.00 FOR CUST. NO.3103.
10.ACCT. RECEIVABLE BALANCE $ 1915.00 CREDIT LIMIT $ 1000.00 FOR CUST. NO.4101.
10.ACCT. RECEIVABLE BALANCE $ 3575.00 CREDIT LIMIT $ 2000.00 FOR CUST. NO.4102.
10.ACCT. RECEIVABLE BALANCE $ 1070.00 CREDIT LIMIT $ 500.00 FOR CUST. NO.4103.

```
10.ACCT. RECEIVABLE BALANCE $ 1915.00 CREDIT LIMIT $ 1000.00 FOR CUST. NO.5101.
10.ACCT. RECEIVABLE BALANCE $ 3575.00 CREDIT LIMIT $ 2000.00 FOR CUST. NO.5102.
10.ACCT. RECEIVABLE BALANCE $ 1070.00 CREDIT LIMIT $  500.00 FOR CUST. NO.5103.
NUMBER OF EXCEPTIONS IN SAMPLE IS GREATER THAN ACCEPTABLE LIMIT FOR 10
11.COST IS .600 PERCENT OF SELLING PRICE FOR PART NO. 1006. VALUE $   150.00
11.COST IS .928 PERCENT OF SELLING PRICE FOR PART NO. 1008. VALUE $    48.72
11.COST IS .620 PERCENT OF SELLING PRICE FOR PART NO. 1100. VALUE $    37.20
11.COST IS .600 PERCENT OF SELLING PRICE FOR PART NO. 1130. VALUE $    60.00
11.COST IS .600 PERCENT OF SELLING PRICE FOR PART NO. 3006. VALUE $   150.00
11.COST IS .928 PERCENT OF SELLING PRICE FOR PART NO. 3008. VALUE $    48.72
11.COST IS .620 PERCENT OF SELLING PRICE FOR PART NO. 3100. VALUE $    37.20
11.COST IS .600 PERCENT OF SELLING PRICE FOR PART NO. 3130. VALUE $    60.00
11.COST IS .600 PERCENT OF SELLING PRICE FOR PART NO. 4006. VALUE $   150.00
11.COST IS .928 PERCENT OF SELLING PRICE FOR PART NO. 4008. VALUE $    48.72
11.COST IS .620 PERCENT OF SELLING PRICE FOR PART NO. 4100. VALUE $    37.20
11.COST IS .600 PERCENT OF SELLING PRICE FOR PART NO. 4130. VALUE $    60.00
11.COST IS .600 PERCENT OF SELLING PRICE FOR PART NO. 5006. VALUE $   150.00
11.COST IS .928 PERCENT OF SELLING PRICE FOR PART NO. 5008. VALUE $    48.72
11.COST IS .620 PERCENT OF SELLING PRICE FOR PART NO. 5100. VALUE $    37.20
11.COST IS .600 PERCENT OF SELLING PRICE FOR PART NO. 5130. VALUE $    60.00
NUMBER OF EXCEPTIONS IN SAMPLE IS GREATER THAN ACCEPTABLE LIMIT FOR 11
9. ENDING INVENTORY ERROR FOR PART NO.1111. OF    2. UNITS $  160.00
9. ENDING INVENTORY ERROR FOR PART NO.1114. OF    1. UNITS $  150.00
9. ENDING INVENTORY ERROR FOR PART NO.1116. OF    1. UNITS $  122.00
9. ENDING INVENTORY ERROR FOR PART NO.1117. OF    3. UNITS $  132.00
9. ENDING INVENTORY ERROR FOR PART NO.3111. OF    2. UNITS $  160.00
9. ENDING INVENTORY ERROR FOR PART NO.3114. OF    1. UNITS $  150.00
9. ENDING INVENTORY ERROR FOR PART NO.3116. OF    1. UNITS $  122.00
9. ENDING INVENTORY ERROR FOR PART NO.3117. OF    3. UNITS $  132.00
9. ENDING INVENTORY ERROR FOR PART NO.4002. OF    6. UNITS $   18.00
9. ENDING INVENTORY ERROR FOR PART NO.4111. OF    2. UNITS $  160.00
9. ENDING INVENTORY ERROR FOR PART NO.4114. OF    1. UNITS $  150.00
9. ENDING INVENTORY ERROR FOR PART NO.4116. OF    1. UNITS $  122.00
9. ENDING INVENTORY ERROR FOR PART NO.4117. OF    3. UNITS $  132.00
9. ENDING INVENTORY ERROR FOR PART NO.5111. OF    2. UNITS $  160.00
9. ENDING INVENTORY ERROR FOR PART NO.5114. OF    1. UNITS $  150.00
9. ENDING INVENTORY ERROR FOR PART NO.5116. OF    1. UNITS $  122.00
9. ENDING INVENTORY ERROR FOR PART NO.5117. OF    3. UNITS $  132.00
NUMBER OF EXCEPTIONS IN SAMPLE IS GREATER THAN ACCEPTABLE LIMIT FOR  9
14.COMPUTED ENDING A/R BALANCE EXCEEDS BALANCE FOR CUST. NO.2115. BY $   74.85
14.BALANCE EXCEEDS COMPUTED ENDING A/R BALANCE FOR CUST. NO.2119. BY $  183.00
14.COMPUTED ENDING A/R BALANCE EXCEEDS BALANCE FOR CUST. NO.2120. BY $  183.00
14.BALANCE EXCEEDS COMPUTED ENDING A/R BALANCE FOR CUST. NO.3000. BY $   12.00
14.COMPUTED ENDING A/R BALANCE EXCEEDS BALANCE FOR CUST. NO.3115. BY $   74.85
14.BALANCE EXCEEDS COMPUTED ENDING A/R BALANCE FOR CUST. NO.3119. BY $  183.00
14.COMPUTED ENDING A/R BALANCE EXCEEDS BALANCE FOR CUST. NO.3120. BY $  183.00
14.BALANCE EXCEEDS COMPUTED ENDING A/R BALANCE FOR CUST. NO.4010. BY $   24.00
14.COMPUTED ENDING A/R BALANCE EXCEEDS BALANCE FOR CUST. NO.4115. BY $   74.85
14.BALANCE EXCEEDS COMPUTED ENDING A/R BALANCE FOR CUST. NO.4119. BY $  183.00
14.COMPUTED ENDING A/R BALANCE EXCEEDS BALANCE FOR CUST. NO.4120. BY $  183.00
14.COMPUTED ENDING A/R BALANCE EXCEEDS BALANCE FOR CUST. NO.5115. BY $   74.85
14.BALANCE EXCEEDS COMPUTED ENDING A/R BALANCE FOR CUST. NO.5119. BY $  183.00
14.COMPUTED ENDING A/R BALANCE EXCEEDS BALANCE FOR CUST. NO.5120. BY $  183.00
NUMBER OF EXCEPTIONS IN SAMPLE IS GREATER THAN ACCEPTABLE LIMIT FOR 14
15. DETAIL AMOUNTS EXCEED DEBITS POSTED TO CONTROL ACCOUNT BY $  263.40
```

Bibliography

BOOKS

Ackoff, Russell L., ed. *Progress in Operations Research.* New York: John Wiley & Sons, 1951. 505 pp.

Babbage, Charles. *Passages from the Life of a Philosopher.* London: Longman, Green, Longman, Roberts & Green, 1864. 496 pp.

Babbage, Henry P., ed. *Babbage's Calculating Engines, Being a Collection of Papers Relating to Them, Their History and Construction.* London: E. and F. N. Spon, 1889. 342 pp.

Barish, Norman N. *Systems Analysis for Effective Administration.* New York: Funk & Wagnalls, 1951. 316 pp.

Baumol, William J. *Economic Dynamics.* 2d ed. New York: The Macmillan Company, 1959. 396 pp.

Bell, William D. *A Management Guide to Electronic Computers.* New York: McGraw-Hill Book Company, 1957. 403 pp.

Berkeley, Edmund C. *Giant Brains or Machines That Think.* New York: John Wiley & Sons, 1949. 294 pp.

Borko, Harold, ed. *Computer Applications in the Behavioral Sciences.* Englewood Cliffs, N. J.: Prentice-Hall, 1962. 633 pp.

Boulding, Kenneth E. *Economic Analysis.* 3d ed. New York: Harper & Brothers, 1955. 905 pp.

Brooks, Frederick P., Jr., and Kenneth E. Iverson. *Automatic Data Processing.* New York: John Wiley & Sons, 1963. 494 pp.

Burton, A. J., and R. G. Mills. *Electronic Computers and Their Business Applications.* London: Ernest Benn Ltd., 1960. 325 pp.

Canning, Richard G. *Electronic Data Processing for Business and Industry.* New York: John Wiley & Sons, 1956. 332 pp.

———. *Installing Electronic Data Processing Systems.* New York: John Wiley & Sons, 1957. 193 pp.

Chapin, Ned. *An Introduction to Automatic Computers.* 2d ed. Princeton, N. J.: D. Van Nostrand Company, 1963. 503 pp.

———. *Programming Computers for Business Applications.* New York: McGraw-Hill Book Company, 1961. 279 pp.

Cyert, R. M., and H. Justin Davidson. *Statistical Sampling for Accounting Information.* Englewood Cliffs, N. J.: Prentice-Hall, 1962. 224 pp.

Dean, Joel. *Managerial Economics.* Englewood Cliffs, N. J.: Prentice-Hall, 1951. 621 pp.

Dickey, Robert I., ed. *Accountants' Cost Handbook.* 2d ed. New York: Ronald Press, 1960. 1002 pp.

Dicksee, Lawrence R. *Auditing.* London: Gee & Co., 1905. 385 pp.

Edwards, James Don. *History of Public Accounting in the United States.* East Lansing, Michigan: Bureau of Business and Economic Research, Graduate School of Business Administration, Michigan State University, 1960. 368 pp.

Goode, H. Machal. *System Engineering*. McGraw-Hill Book Company, 1957. 551 pp.

Greenberger, Martin, ed. *Management and the Computer of the Future*. New York: John Wiley & Sons, 1962. 340 pp.

Gregory, Robert H., and Richard Van Horn. *Automatic Data Processing Systems, Principles and Procedures*. 2d ed. San Francisco, Calif.: Wadsworth Publishing Company, 1963. 816 pp.

Grielink, A. B. *Auditing Automatic Data Processing*. Amsterdam: Elsevier Publishing Company, 1961. 68 pp.

Haire, Mason, ed. *Modern Organization Theory*. New York: John Wiley & Sons, 1959. 324 pp.

Halstead, Maurice H. *Machine-Independent Computer Programming*. Washington, D. C.: Spartan Books, 1962. 267 pp.

Hartree, Douglas R. *Calculating Instruments and Machines*. Urbana, Ill.: University of Illinois Press, 1949. 137 pp.

Hein, Leonard W. *An Introduction to Electronic Data Processing for Business*. Princeton, N. J.: D. Van Nostrand Company, 1961. 320 pp.

Holmes, Arthur W. *Basic Auditing Principles*. Homewood, Ill.: Richard D. Irwin, 1962. 370 pp.

Johnson, Eldred A. *Accounting Systems in Modern Business*. New York: McGraw-Hill Book Company, 1959. 453 pp.

Johnson, James T., and J. Herman Brasseaux. *Readings in Auditing*. Cincinnati, Ohio: South-Western Publishing Company, 1960. 658 pp.

Kaufman, Felix. *Electronic Data Processing and Auditing*. New York: Ronald Press, 1961. 180 pp.

Kozmetsky, George, and Paul Kircher. *Electronic Computers and Management Control*. New York: McGraw-Hill Book Company, 1956. 296 pp.

Laden, H. N., and T. R. Gildersleeve. *System Design for Computer Applications*. New York: John Wiley & Sons, 1963. 330 pp.

Leeds, Herbert D., and Gerald M. Weinberg. *Computer Programming Fundamentals*. New York: McGraw-Hill Book Company, 1961. 368 pp.

Likert, Rensis. *New Patterns of Management*. New York: McGraw-Hill Book Company, 1961. 279 pp.

Littleton, A. C. *Accounting Evolution to 1900*. New York: American Institute Publishing Company, 1933. 368 pp.

McCracken, Daniel D., Harold Weiss, and Tsai-Hwa Lee. *Programming Business Computers*. New York: John Wiley & Sons, 1959. 510 pp.

Martin, E. Wainwright, Jr. *Electronic Data Processing—An Introduction*. Homewood, Ill.: Richard D. Irwin, 1961. 423 pp.

Mautz, R. K., and H. A. Sharaf. *The Philosophy of Auditing*. Menasha, Wisc.: American Accounting Association, 1961. 248 pp.

Meigs, Walter B. *Principles of Auditing*. Homewood, Ill.: Richard D. Irwin, 1962. 820 pp.

Mittman, Benjamin, and Andrew Ungar. *Computer Applications*. New York: The Macmillan Company, 1960. 193 pp.

Montgomery, Robert H. *Auditing Theory and Practice*. New York: Ronald Press, 1912. 673 pp.

Montgomery's "Auditing." New York: Ronald Press, 1957. 766 pp.

Murphy, Gordon J. *Basic Automatic Control Theory*. Princeton, N. J.: D. Van Nostrand Company, 1957. 557 pp.

Nelson, Oscar S., and Richard S. Woods. *Accounting Systems and Data Processing.* Cincinnati, Ohio: South-Western Publishing Company, 1961. 643 pp.

Nett, Roger, and Stanley Hetzler. *An Introduction to Electronic Data Processing.* Glencoe, Ill.: The Free Press, 1959. 287 pp.

Neuschel, Richard F. *Management by System.* 2d ed. New York: McGraw-Hill Book Company, 1960. 359 pp.

Oakford, Robert V. *Introduction to Electronic Data Processing Equipment.* New York: McGraw-Hill Book Company, 1962. 340 pp.

Peloubet, Sidney W., and Herbert Heaton. *Integrated Auditing.* New York: Ronald Press, 1958. 272 pp.

Price, Derek, and John DeSolla, *Science Since Babylon.* New Haven, Conn.: Yale University Press, 1961. 149 pp.

Scientific American Editors. *Automatic Control.* New York: Simon & Schuster, 1955. 149 pp.

Shannon, Claude E., and Warren Weaver. *The Mathematical Theory of Communication.* Urbana, Ill.: University of Illinois Press, 1949. 117 pp.

Siegelman, Louis, and Milton H. Spencer. *Managerial Economics.* Homewood, Ill.: Richard D. Irwin, 1959. 454 pp.

Simon, Herbert A. *The New Science of Management Decision.* New York: Harper & Brothers, 1960. 50 pp.

———. *Administrative Behavior.* New York: The Macmillan Company, 1958. 259 pp.

Smith, Ed Sinclair. *Automatic Control Engineering.* New York: McGraw-Hill Book Company, 1944. 367 pp.

Sprague, Richard E. *Electronic Business Systems.* New York: Ronald Press, 1962. 168 pp.

Stettler, Howard A. *Auditing Principles.* Englewood Cliffs, N. J.: Prentice-Hall, 1961. 746 pp.

Thomas, William E., ed. *Readings in Cost Accounting, Budgeting, and Control.* Cincinnati, Ohio: South-Western Publishing Company, 1955. 784 pp. Published for the American Accounting Association.

Tustin, Arnold. *The Mechanism of Economic Systems.* Cambridge, Mass.: Harvard University Press, 1953. 161 pp.

Vatter, William J. *Managerial Accounting.* Englewood Cliffs, N. J.: Prentice-Hall, 1950. 510 pp.

Wallace, Frank. *Appraising the Economics of Electronic Computers.* New York: Controllership Foundation, 1956. 106 pp.

Wiener, Norbert. *Cybernetics.* New York: McGraw-Hill Book Company, 1961. 194 pp.

Wolins, Martin, director. *A Manual for Cost Analysis in Residential Institutions for Children.* Berkeley, California: California State Department of Social Welfare and Child Welfare League of America, Inc., 1962. 60 pp.

MONOGRAPHS AND ARTICLES

American Institute of Accountants. *Audits of Corporate Accounts.* New York: The Institute, 1934. 36 pp.

———. *Internal Control.* New York: The Institute, 1949. 24 pp.

———. *Verification of Financial Statements.* Rev. ed. Washington, D. C.: Federal Reserve Board, 1929. 34 pp.

American Institute of Certified Public Accountants. "Report of Committee on Electronic Accounting" (April, 1957); condensed in *Annual Report of the American Institute of Certified Public Accountants*. New York: The Institute, 1947. 23 pp.

———. *Generally Accepted Auditing Standards, Their Significance and Scope*. New York: The Institute, 1954. 54 pp.

———. *Scope of the Independent Auditor's Review of Internal Control*. New York: The Institute, 1954. 34 pp.

American Management Association. *The Changing Dimensions of Office Management*. Management Report No. 41. New York: The Association, 1960. 159 pp.

———. *Data Processing Today: A Progress Report*. Management Report No. 46. New York: The Association, 1960. 143 pp.

Balderston, F. E. *Optimal and Feasible Choices in Organizations Having Multiple Goals*. Working Paper No. 12, Management Sciences Nucleus, Institute of Industrial Relations, University of California. Berkeley, Calif.: The Institute, February, 1960.

Blank, Virgil. "Electronic Data Processing Programming for the Internal Auditor," *The Internal Auditor*, XVI (March, 1959), 16-22.

———. "The Management Concept in Electronic Systems," *The Journal of Accountancy*, 111 (January, 1961), 59-66.

Boni, Gregory M. "Impact of EDP on Auditing," *The Journal of Accountancy*, 116 (September, 1963), 48-53.

Boulding, Kenneth E. "General Systems Theory—Skeleton of Science," *Management Science*, 2 (April, 1956), 197-202.

Boutell, Wayne S. "Business-Oriented Computers: A Frame of Reference," *Accounting Review*, XXXIX (April, 1964), 305-311.

———. "The Implementation of Uniform Standards of Reporting for National Voluntary Agencies," *Accounting Review*, XXXVIII (July, 1962), 406-409.

Boyce, L. Fred, Jr. "Installing a Medium-Sized Computer," *The Journal of Accountancy*, 110 (July, 1960), 48-53.

Cadematori, Kenneth G. "Internal Control Audit Trail and Electronics," *The New York Certified Public Accountant*, XXIX (June, 1959), 426-438.

Campbell, Robert V. D. "Evolution of Automatic Computation," *Proceedings of the Association for Computing Machinery*. Pittsburgh: Richard Rimbach Associates, 1952. 15 pp.

Chase, Charles G. "Why the Automatic Office is Still Some Years Off," *The Office*, XLI (January, 1955), 84-88.

Cleaver, Goodrich F. "Auditing and Electronic Data Processing," *The Journal of Accountancy*, 106 (November, 1958), 48-54.

Connolly, James J. "Case Study of a Computer Audit Program" *The Price Waterhouse Review*, VII (Winter, 1963), 42-46.

Corcoran, A. Wayne, and Donald F. Istvan. *The Audit and the Punched Card, An Introduction*. Bureau of Business Research, Research Monograph No. 101. Columbus, Ohio: The Ohio State University, 1961. 75 pp.

Coulson, H. O. H. "Mechanized Accounting; Auditing Procedure," *The Accountant*, CXXVII (November 22, 1952), 610-616.

Curka, Frank J. "The Effect of Electronic Data Processing on Auditing," *National Association of Accountants Bulletin*, XLII (April, 1961), 85-91.

Davies, William R. "Management Progresses in Its Use of Internal Audit Control," *The Office,* XLVII (January, 1958), 90-100.

Ernst and Ernst. *Establishing an Integrated Data-Processing System,* American Management Association Special Report No. 11. New York: The Association, 1956. 183 pp.

Frielink, A. B. *Auditing Automatic Data Processing.* Amsterdam: Elsevier Publishing Company, 1961. 68 pp.

Gallagher, James D. *Management Information Systems and the Computer.* American Management Association Research Report No. 51. New York: The Association, 1961. 191 pp.

Garland, Robert F. "Five Ways in Which Computer Systems Strengthen Internal Control" *National Association of Accountants Bulletin,* XLIII (July, 1962), 21-28.

Grody, Charles E. "The Auditor Encounters Computers," *The Internal Auditor,* XVI (March, 1959), 31-34.

Guest, L. D., Jr. *Administrative Automation of Sylvania: Centralized Data Processing, Decentralized Management.* American Management Association Office Management Series No. 144. New York: The Association, 1956. 72 pp.

Hamman, Paul E. "The Audit of Machine Records," *The Journal of Accountancy,* 101 (March, 1956), 56-61.

Haskins and Sells, *Introduction to Data Processing.* New York: Haskins and Sells Publication, 1957. 107 pp.

Hoag, Malcolm W. "What is a System?" *Operations Research,* V (June, 1957), 445-449.

Holland, Ray L. "The Audit of a Punched Card Accounting Installation," *The Internal Auditor,* XII (March, 1956), 20-25.

Hoos, Ida R. "When the Computer Takes Over the Office," *Harvard Business Review,* 37 (July-August, 1960), 102-112.

International Business Machines Corporation. *The Auditor Encounters Electronic Data Processing.* Prepared by Price Waterhouse & Co. New York: IBM Corporation, 1956. 24 pp.

———. *In-line Electronic Accounting, Internal Control and Audit Trail.* Prepared by Price Waterhouse & Co. New York: IBM Corporation, 1958. 9 pp.

Jauchem, C. R. "Impact of Electronic Data Processing on Auditing," *National Association of Accountants Bulletin,* XXXIX (May, 1958), 53-59.

———. "The Importance of Controls in Electronic Data-Processing," *The Federal Accountant,* VII (September, 1957), 38-43.

Kaufman, Felix. "EDP Control Problems," *The Controller,* July, 1962, pp. 364-366.

Kaufman, Felix, and L. A. Schmidt. "Auditing Electronic Records," in James T. Johnson and J. Herman Brasseaux, eds., *Readings in Auditing.* Cincinnati, Ohio: South-Western Publishing Company, 1960. Pp. 560-571.

Leavitt, H. J., and T. L. Whisler. "Management in the 1980's," *Harvard Business Review,* 36 (November-December, 1958), 41-48.

Lewis, Ralph F. "The C.P.A. Views Mechanized Accounting," *The Controller,* September, 1956, pp. 405-408.

McCullough, T. E. "The Auditor Uses the Computer," *The Internal Auditor,* XVI (December, 1959), 34-38.

MacDonald, W. L. "The Auditor and the Computer," *The Canadian Chartered Accountant,* September, 1962, pp. 256-260.

Margetts, J. W. "The Auditor and the Computer. From a Statutory Auditor's Viewpoint," *The Accountant,* CXXXIX (September 6, 1958), 276-283.

Moyer, C. A. "Early Developments in American Auditing," *Accounting Review,* XXXVI (January, 1951), 3-8.

Murray, J. R. "Auditing Electronically Produced Record," *The Canadian Chartered Accountant,* February, 1957, pp. 117-124.

Nau, Carl H. "The American Institute of Accountants," *The Journal of Accountancy,* 31 (February, 1921), 103-109.

Oberfell, J. W. "Case Study of a Computer Audit Program in Action," *The Price Waterhouse Review,* VI (Summer, 1961), 40-48.

Paddock, Harold E. "Some Audit Aspects of Punched Card and Electronic Data Processing," *The Internal Auditor,* XVI (June, 1959), 38-50.

Palmer, R. E. "The Changing Role of the Internal Auditor," *The Accountant's Journal,* XLVII (October, 1955), 279-282.

Pelij, Joseph. "How Will Business Electronics Affect the Auditor's Work?" *The Journal of Accountancy,* 117 (July, 1964), 36-44.

Perry, George M. "The Nature of Computer Control," *The Internal Auditor,* XVI (December, 1959), 29-33.

Pfenning, R. E. "Business Information Systems," *Accounting Review,* XXXVII (April, 1962), 234-243.

Puder, Richard K. "Local Practitioners Can Use Computers," *The Journal of Accountancy,* 114 (July, 1962), 47-52.

Salveson, M. E. "Computers in the Design of Business Organizations," in American Management Association, *Electronics in Action,* Special Report No. 22. New York: The Association, 1957. 129 pp.

Seitz, Phillip. "Auditing Electronic Data-Processing Systems," *The Illinois Certified Public Accountant,* No. 17 (July, 1955), 42-48.

Shipley, E. T. "The Auditor's Job in the Computer Era," *Banking,* LI (March, 1959), 46, 130.

Shonting, C. M., and L. D. Stone. "Audit Techniques for Electronic Systems," in James T. Johnson and J. Herman Brasseaux, *Readings in Auditing.* Cincinnatti Ohio: South-Western Publishing Company, 1960. Pp. 572-584.

Spellman, John R. "Auditing the EDP System," *The Arthur Andersen Chronicle,* 22 (April, 1962), 54-67.

Stonier, Brian. "Impact of Computers on Auditing," *The Chartered Accountant in Australia,* 30 (September, 1959), 154-157.

Toan, A. B., Jr. "Auditing, Control, and Electronics," in James T. Johnson and J. Herman Brasseaux, *Readings in Auditing.* Cincinnati, Ohio: South-Western Publishing Company, 1960. Pp. 550-559.

————. "The Auditor and EDP," *The Journal of Accountancy,* 109 (June 1960), 42-46.

Trombly, Robert N. "Auditing Through EDP Equipment," *National Association of Accountants Bulletin,* XCII (May, 1961), 67-72.

United States Air Force. *Guide for Auditing Automatic Data Processing Systems,* Washington, D. C.: U. S. Government Printing Office, 1961. 134 pp.

Vance, Lawrence L. "A Review of Developments in Statistical Sampling for Accountants," *Accounting Review,* XXXV (January, 1960), 19-28.

Vannais, Leon E. "Punched Card Accounting From the Audit Viewpoint," *The Journal of Accountancy,* 70 (September, 1940), 200-217; (October, 1940), 339-356.

Wallace, Edward L. *Management Influence in the Design of Data-Processing Systems: A Case Study.* Boston: Division of Research, Graduate School of Business Administration, Harvard University, 1961. 259 pp.

Weiss, Harold. "The Programmer Encounters Auditing," *Datamation,* 9 (September, 1963), 31-34.

Whitmer, William E. "Electronic Data Processing, Its Effect on the Auditor," *The Arthur Young Journal,* January, 1961, pp. 17-24.

Williams, E. C. R., and D. J. Bailey. "Application of Data-Processing Equipment in the Office," *The Accountant,* CXXXV (November 3, 1956), 455-460.

Woods, Richard S. "The Development of Auditing Standards and Techniques for EDP Systems," *National Association of Accountants Bulletin,* 43 (September, 1961), 27-48.

Wright, Robert G. "Changing Concepts in EDP Feasibility Studies," *The Journal of Accountancy* 113 (June, 1962), 47-51.

Lightning Source UK Ltd.
Milton Keynes UK
UKHW012356220722
406246UK00005B/485